Charlie
& Me

CHARLIE AND ME
First published 2011
by New Island
2 Brookside
Dundrum Road
Dublin 14
www.newisland.ie

Copyright © Catherine Barry, 2011
The author has asserted her moral rights.

ISBN 978-1- 8484-0090-0
British Library Cataloguing Data. A CIP catalogue record for this book is
available from the British Library.

Internal design by Liberties Press
Cover design by www.sinedesign.net
Printed and bound in the UK by CPI Antony Rowe, Chippenham and
Eastbourne.

New Island re   ved financial assistance from
The Arts Cou   l (An Co   ation), Dublin, Ireland

Charlie
& Me

A true story

Catherine Barry

NEW
ISLAND

For my father, John Francis Barry

In April 1993 I found myself sitting in my first Alcoholics Anonymous meeting. It was a blustery night, and I had almost not made it. I had visited my doctor two days before and said the dreaded words, for the first time: 'I think I might have a bit of a drinking problem.' Only a teeny-weeny one, mind you, ever so slight.

Alcoholism – being, infamously, the only disease that tells you you haven't got it – still had me in a headlock of chronic denial. Looking back, I don't know how I actually got to the meeting. It had been a toss-up whether I would hit the pub or the meeting. I paused briefly outside the pub. I was being simultaneously assaulted by two opposite inclinations. Have a drink. Don't have a drink. Have a drink. Don't have a drink. The trademark 'see-sawing' of the addict's addled mind was in full and truculent swing.

Then something extraordinary happened. Like an invisible policeman, something outside of myself moved me on from the pub. I was pushed away by some unknown force. I remember thinking: what am I doing? My mind was venturing down one road while my legs were stubbornly insisting on taking me down another. They took me to a door which, when opened, would change my life.

I put my trembling hand on the doorknob, twisted it and walked inside. I had no idea what to expect, was petrified, and was still unsure about why I was there. I sat on my hands on a hard-backed chair, as people swirled about me, chatting, laughing and clattering cups and saucers.

I was shaking badly. I hadn't had a drink for four days, but the shakes had started only that day. I put it down to nerves about the meeting. Those present all looked much older than me, and most of them were male. I searched the room for someone of my age. I was thirty years old and keenly felt how young I was to be there. I was bankrupt, spiritually, mentally and physically. I was eight and a half stone and hadn't eaten properly for two years. Being in the room just didn't feel right. I couldn't chew, let alone swallow the huge piece of humble pie that was my admittance fee into the 'Well and truly fucked-up beyond any chance of redemption' club which I perceived to be Alcoholics Anonymous. That I was destined to sit in a stinking room of middle-aged and old men jabbering on about their drinking careers and lying about how they had achieved a 'life beyond their wildest dreams' without booze, was beyond my grain-of-rice-sized brain.

I got up to leave before the meeting started. I had just made it to the door when a soft hand landed on my shoulder. I turned around and a small, slim man, with startling blue eyes and a hat, was smiling at me. It was a clownish, auspicious type of grin. Think Norman Wisdom, with a smattering of Tommy Cooper thrown in the mix.

'I'm Charlie,' the man said.

'I'm Cathy,' I managed.

'Welcome home, Cathy,' he said, smiling.

He put out his hand. I shook it. It was firm, reassuring; it contained something inexplicably familiar. When our hands touched, a vibrant current of warmth coursed through my veins. I recognised the sensation, the connectedness. Overwhelmed with an inexorable sadness, I realised that it was life that had surged through me, and I knew there and then that I had been sleeping for a very long time.

Charlie led me back inside. My new life began.

The following is an account of Charlie Gallagher, the man in the hat, who became my sponsor in Alcoholics Anonymous. A sponsor acts as a mirror, a sounding board. It's someone who has walked the path of recovery and is willing to pass on the message to the novice. Having sponsored people myself, I know how tough this emotional contract can be. The job specification involves unconditional commitment and Job-like patience. A ready ear and a non-judgmental heart are essential. You don't get any holidays and, worse still, you don't get paid, but nothing guarantees continued personal sobriety more than helping the newcomer.

Charlie Gallagher graciously imparted his wisdom, warmth and sense of humour to me. His attitude towards life and all its inherent potholes gave me a blueprint – an instruction book on decent living, if you like. His help was, and still is, invaluable. Perhaps in reading his truth, you too might find some 'jewels in the mud'.

1

How did I get to Alcoholics Anonymous?

It was a stockpile of serendipitous incidents. In 1993 two of my heroes were in Dublin to give concerts: Peter Gabriel and Bruce Springsteen. I was financially on skid row at the time and had to scrape together the money to buy tickets, but I couldn't afford the luxury of both, so I had to choose which concert to go to. I chose Bruce Springsteen: after all, I had waited twenty years to see him. At the same time, I was yearning to see Peter Gabriel.

After seeing Bruce and being slightly disappointed with the performance (I know, I know, how could anyone be disappointed with a Bruce Springsteen concert?), I couldn't stop thinking about the Peter Gabriel gig that was coming up four days later. I felt I'd made the wrong decision. My partner at the time, knowing how much I wanted to see Peter Gabriel, arrived home early from work on the eve of the concert with two tickets. I was ill with excitement – ecstatic, to say the least – and simply couldn't wait to see Gabriel live. I was (and am) a huge fan. I could barely contain myself and, as always when stimulated to such a feverish pitch, I began drinking earlier than usual. I was two sheets to the wind before I even left home.

The Point Theatre was jammed. The stage set-up was yin and yang: two separate podiums, one at either end of the hall, representing the male and female. The two platforms were connected by a moving conveyor belt that served as an emblematic communication line between the sexes. The whole show centred on Gabriel's new album *The Secret World*, a study of relationships. I had always seen him as a real artist, a sculptor who had completely mastered his craft. He is more than just a singer/songwriter: he is someone who endeavours to translate stories into vividly dramatic and accessible live performances. He has the uncanny ability to transform a song into a play, acting out the songs, taking the lead role; his musicians are accompanying thespians, and his audience are the extras. His genius for taking music and inflating it with life before your very eyes is legendary. To me, he is primarily a storyteller, and this concert was a phantasmagorical voyage into the psyche of the human heart.

I stood very close to the stage, not more than six feet away from the man himself. He arrived on stage in white pyjamas – barefoot, solemn, commanding and enigmatic. Even now, in his fifties, with his snow-white hair and goatee, he exudes a raw, Sean Connery sexual potency. Of course everyone's taste is different, but for me the man is perversely carnal: eroticism and sensuality ooze out of every steamy pore. And those cat-green piercing eyes! I would be only too happy to yield to their intense, hypnotic calling and administer to his every filthy, debauched whim. He's got that certain something, a blend of evil menace and Peter Pan-like vulnerability, two qualities that grind off each other in a way that simply should not work. It's like mixing oil and water; but between the two extremes, you find something liberating and identifiable. It's his humanity and understanding of it, the way he exposes it in all its captivating beauty and devastating imperfections. So anyone attending a Peter Gabriel concert undergoes a kind of soul surgery.

That night, he operated on me.

He sang about communication ('Come talk to me', with a guest appearance from the amazing Sinéad O'Connor); he sang about emotional pain and trying to face old ghosts ('Digging in the dirt'); and by the time he got to the track 'Secret world' itself, I started to weep. He was singing those words to *me*. I understood them, not through my ears, but through some spiritual valve in my heart. I had been hiding out in pubs, pints and small ones. What had I been thinking of? Who was I fooling? My life was a shambles. I had broken relationships coming out of my ears. I had failed to achieve any of my dreams. The only thing I had managed to do consistently was change my mind. I had abandoned myself. Any semblance of accountability, self-respect, dignity or principle – qualities that were an integral part of the person I had once called 'me' – had ceased to exist. The sinking ship had gone down and I hadn't even donned a life jacket.

In short, I hated me. I despised what I had become.

I was a mother of two children (fathered by two different men), living with one of them, who was a detestable man, in a part of Dublin I loathed, and working in a job that was wholly unsuitable. My life was a sham. I was not who I wanted to be, and I was awash with toxic shame.

In the Point Theatre, I stared at the pint in my hand. Suddenly, the very sight of it sickened me. I tipped the plastic cup forward, allowing the remains to trickle slowly to the floor. That was effectively the end of my drinking days. It was my spiritual awakening, although I didn't know that then. I walked home from the concert rocked to stony silence, thinking, thinking.

I travelled back over the years, stopping at various junctions and crossroads, pinpointing where it had all begun to unravel. The missed opportunities, the smashed relationships, the reneged-on promises, the devastating loneliness, the disappointments, the heartache all passed before my eyes. I was in my own private garden of Gethsemane but, unlike Jesus, I knew the only person who had betrayed me was me.

By the time I got home, I was stone-cold sober. I sat all night on the side of the bed, gazing out of the window. It was as if someone had lifted the veil: something extraordinary had happened to me at that concert. A juggernaut of truth had managed to bulldoze its way through my fortified heart, and I knew with pristine clarity what I had to do.

The next day, I went to see my doctor.

The following week, I hit Alcoholics Anonymous.

My state of mind was still savage. How was I going to rectify twenty years of doing the wrong thing? I didn't know where to start. I wonder if, had Charlie Gallagher not followed me as I'd tried to escape from that first meeting, I would have mustered up the courage to go back. Charlie was twenty-six years sober at the time, and as many years older than me. He knew exactly what I was trying to do. He knew the disease was desperate to keep me in its grip. He knew it was talking to me, telling me to get away from the meeting as fast as I could.

However, I got through it – though I don't remember much of it. I was such a nervous wreck, and so confused, I didn't take anything in. I just knew there was something in the participants with which I could identify. I wanted what they had. I wanted that glint in the eye, that spark of life, which I witnessed all around me, even though I was suspicious of everyone.

Charlie offered to sponsor me. I didn't know what the word 'sponsor' meant. He explained that he would simply pass on the tools of recovery to me as they had been passed on to him twenty-five years earlier. In short, he would show me how to get, and stay, sober. I read the Twelve Steps of Alcoholics Anonymous displayed on the wall, and gasped. Admit defeat. Turn your life over to a higher power. Make amends to those you have hurt, and so on. How would I manage any of those? Charlie reassured me that the Twelve Steps were not important to me at that moment. What was important was that I attend meetings daily, that I did not drink in between them, and that I would pick up the phone to him if I felt I was going to take a drink. He said it was that simple. I didn't believe him, but I wanted to, and that was my saving grace.

For the next two years, I went to an AA meeting seven evenings a week. Luckily, I had found myself a kind and reliable babysitter to look after my children while I attended to the business of getting well. I found a local meeting, and it soon became my anchor group. On Wednesday and Saturday evenings, Charlie and I went to other AA meetings together. I looked forward to hearing the familiar beep-beep of his car outside my front door.

Charlie had a penchant for banjaxed cars. We're talking the Flintstones here. The more dilapidated and ramshackle, the better. He couldn't get enough of beat-up old bangers. Often the battery went dead or a hubcap rolled off of its own accord. Many's the time the jalopies simply broke down, inconveniently hissing and spitting their last breath in the middle of a busy motorway.

In 1993, he was driving an old Datsun. It had cost him a hefty £50. It was a hideous turd-brown colour, and had as much va-va-voom as a Perspex jug. Still, it was Charlie's baby. We christened it 'The Brown Rat', even though I had wanted to call it 'Noah's Ark'. The windows didn't go up properly, so when it rained, the car leaked constantly. I had to sit on a pile of plastic bags in what passed for the front seat. If it was raining, I would put my feet up on the dashboard, because the bottom of the car would fill with water.

One day I brought an umbrella and tried to put it up in the car – which Charlie took as an insult. He said if I didn't like it, I could walk. I stayed put, my clutched knees touching my chin, my Dunnes Stores plastic bags crunching under my arse, and my daughter's pink, plastic Barbie rain hat perched on my head.

Charlie would put the key into the ignition, curse and swear, and eventually the engine would splutter into action. Off we would go, the hapless exhaust pipe belching out putrid smoke, the pitiful engine groaning between stops and starts. Frequently, I would have to get out and enlist the help of strangers to give the car a push-start, all the time enduring their contemptuous stares and sneers. The Travelling Wilburys? Not exactly. More like Wilma and Fred.

When you got in the car, you were almost certain to find yourself impaled and/or mutilated by an assortment of jagged-ended artefacts. Charlie collected junk – except he never saw it as junk. He referred to his bric-à-brac as '*objets d'art*'. One day, while we were having a cup of tea in my parents' house, my Dad innocently asked him: 'Charlie, what do you actually do?'

'I'm in sales.'

'Oh? What do you sell?'

'Antiques,' Charlie answered, quite convincingly.

The 'antiques' consisted of rusted wrenches, nuts and bolts, disused cutlery, broken machine parts, half-filled pots of paint, old rags and cast-offs – just about anything that was worthless. He sold his stash at local weekend car boot sales. Why anyone ever bought anything from Charlie is beyond me. It was just garbage.

'It's crap, Charlie,' I would point out.

He was quick to remark that what I termed 'crap' could be viewed by another as an 'Aladdin's cave'. The fact that he did manage to make a paltry sum of money this way bears testimony to his Del Boy charm.

It wasn't unknown for Charlie to jam on the already strained brake pads of the 'Brown Rat' when he spotted a skip on the roadside. He would dash over to it, steal furtive glances around, then climb in and rummage through. Once he came back with a three-wheeler bike.

'Look at this. Imagine throwing out a brand new bike! The waste in this country is shocking; they could have donated that to charity.'

'I'm charity!' I shot up my humble hand.

My daughter was only a year old at the time, so I was thrilled to bits with the bike. Only later did I discover that it had no brakes. Not one to look a gift horse in the mouth, I declined to mention this inconsequential defect to Charlie. Other 'gifts' from him included a child's matching bowl and spoon ('A bit of Parazone and it'll be grand'), a brand new mattress ('Sure, leave it in the garden to air and the damp will go eventually'), a high chair ('It even has its own woodworm; just ignore the little bastards and they'll ignore you'), a battered typewriter ('The "T" and "V" aren't working, but sure you can write them in yourself').

Charlie smoked rolled-up tobacco, either Samson or Drum, and he loved his cigarette. He chain-smoked, but his lungs didn't like it too much. He had a very distinctive cough – a raucous bellow that made him sound like a wounded dinosaur. Often when I went to meetings alone, I would hear the Jurassic Park 'cough', and know that Charlie was in the room. Being a heavy smoker myself, with little or no money, I soon switched to smoking roll-ups.

Charlie was very dapper. He liked to dress up in suits and ties, and he particularly loved hats. That's how he earned the nickname 'The Hat'. He was losing his hair, but that's not why he wore the hats. He wore them because he loved them, and he wore them well. They were usually trilbies of various colours, feathered and felted. Hats embodied his persona and were his trademark. He likened himself to Frank Sinatra, and often tried to sing like him, but he hadn't a note in his head.

I soon learned to tolerate the horrendously out-of-key renditions. Charlie knew that his singing irritated me, but he got great satisfaction out of winding me up. He liked bright colours, but they clashed, often lending him the image, exuberance and eccentricity of a gay parade. It could be blue trousers, with a green shirt and a yellow tie. Charlie knew he looked ridiculous, but he revelled in it. He recounted how he had gone out one evening, to a dance, in a cream velvet three-piece suit and a brown tie. Charlie thought he was God's gift till his mother remarked: 'You're not seriously going out in that get-up. You look like a bloody chocolate eclair.'

Charlie had his work cut out for him, sponsoring me. I was a difficult student: an intellectual snob who had gathered a lot of information and yet knew nothing about life. I was in all but name dead from the neck down, a virtual head on a plate. I knew all about politics, history, psychology and psychiatry – to me, information was a God in itself – but of the real knowledge of life, I knew precious little.

I hadn't a scrap of humility (often confusing it with humiliation). I was bent with resentment and anger, and riddled with layers of self-justification for being that way. I had been hurt, abandoned, used and betrayed. I was sullen and moody. I was self-pitying and was often volunteering for martyrdom. It was everyone's fault bar my own. I was gobby and self-assured, and was unable to listen to well-meaning advice. Someone once defined the alcoholic as 'an egomaniac with an inferiority complex'. Imagine, if you can, that complex dichotomy. Imagine, yet again, the poor bastard on the receiving end of such a twisted mind. How Charlie never slapped me across the face I don't know. He had the patience of a life insurance policy. I only ever heard him raise his voice once – but more of that later.

After meetings, we would go to the old café on the Clontarf

Road (long since gone), and a variety of other coffee shops, to discuss the events of the day. These chats kept me sober on very difficult days – of which I had many. It soon became painfully apparent that I had to make a lot of alterations to my lifestyle in order to stay on the straight and narrow.

The children were one and five years of age, and I had to employ a babysitter to mind them every evening. It's not unknown for new members to go to three meetings a day in the beginning, so I was doing well. (Ten years later, I actually got a calculator and estimated the debt I had incurred from babysitters. It came to a whopping €32,000. An exorbitant expense, some would think, but had I continued to drink, the cost would have been, without doubt, more than monetary. I would eventually have lost my life pass. In any case, they say what you give out will be in direct proportion to what you get back. I was duly refunded in boomerang style – but I'll leave that story until later.)

I applied myself to the task of getting sober, as if my life depended on it, because deep down I knew it did. Having been blessed at birth with an abundance of steely determination, I began to use it constructively for the first time. I had made up my mind that I was going to do it, and when I make up my mind about something, nothing can deter me. I had often despaired at this character trait of mine, not really comprehending whether it is a liability or an asset. In this case, it saved my skin.

One might ask at this stage why I put my life in the hands of a veritable stranger. After all, I didn't know anything about this man's life. Why did I trust Charlie? It is a question worth pondering, but I still don't know the answer. Providence? Fate? Is there something that conspires to align us to the people who can teach us? Yes, I believe there is. I was meant to meet Charlie.

When the student is ready, the teacher appears, they say. Charlie was sent to teach me, and I was a willing student. I often think of the 'Big Bang' theory when endeavouring to explain my experience. Put simply, meeting Charlie was the 'Big Bang' in my life. We all get these revelations, and every individual is faced with the choice of either shooting the messenger or disarming him. Unknowingly, I had already unpinned the walking grenade I had become. I was a white flag.

There was something about Charlie that was simultaneously challenging and reassuring. When he shook my hand, it was a strong, confident handshake, sincere and full of life. He didn't act as if he had it all sorted, he didn't come across as healed. He didn't pontificate, condescend or Bible-thump. He didn't preach, pretend to know all the answers, or assume a prophet-like status. But they say that God works through the strangest people, and didn't he himself carefully select the social outcasts to be his messengers? Didn't he choose the emotionally crippled, the bockety people, and the repentant sinners to be his own disciples? So, with hindsight, there was nothing strange or untoward about Charlie.

Nevertheless, the man was a walking disaster.

He used to remark that he was the *real* bionic man, not that 'fucking eejit' on the telly. Charlie had incurred so many falls and accidents that his hands and fingers, and even his legs, were more a fusion of metal plates than flesh. He was a clumsy bugger who walked like a crab, scuttling along sideways (a typical Cancer). He was awkward, frequently tripping over things. He fumbled and bumbled his way around; everything about him seemed slightly askew. He was one of the most disorganised men I have ever met, yet within the helter-skelter dysfunction that was his life, he knew exactly where everything was, and what he was doing. It was endearing and amusing to watch it all come together. Charlie operated on a frequency level that was entirely his own. It was his perfectly flawed humanness that appealed to me.

Charlie knew instinctively when to remain silent and when to open fire. He never tried to tell me about the pitfalls; he let me fall into them, so I would learn myself how to avoid them, and, at times, how to climb out of them too. How any human being can watch another do that, and not intervene, is beyond me. But Charlie always knew what was best for me.

Charlie Gallagher was an incredibly good writer. He wrote poetry, short stories and even some radio plays. Some of the short stories were published, but he lacked discipline. Charlie was also a voracious reader. He particularly adored Shakespeare, Shelley and Keats.

True to his nature, he often wrote his untidy scrawlings on the strangest of things, and his spelling and grammar were atrocious. I bought him notebooks, journals and pads of sticky notes, but he never used them. Instead, he would hand me his latest writings on the back of a betting slip, or on a petrol voucher, a Lyons tea coupon or a bit of torn-off cardboard from a cornflakes box. I once found a poem he had written on a square of toilet-roll paper, pinned to the dashboard of his car.

He soon gave me two nicknames – 'The crossword girl' and 'The rotten rip'. If I was being defiant and belligerent (which I was apt to be), he called me 'The rotten rip'. If I was hibernating and evasive, he called me 'The crossword girl'. It was a perfect description of me at the time. Some parts of me were filled in; others were missing. Charlie knew that instinctively. It is also interesting to note that he was the only man I have ever met who noticed that my blue eyes turned green when I got angry.

2

One evening, Charlie and I went to the coffee shop for a post-meeting chat. I had been sober for three months and was as shockingly miserable as ever. I was struggling with my anger and resentment. It had become apparent almost immediately that in order to stay off the booze, I was going to have to leave my marriage. It appeared that all my husband and I had in common in the first instance was our destructive drinking. Now that I didn't drink any more, the family home had become a battleground. I was filled with hatred towards my husband, who was soon to become my ex. I had already instigated legal proceedings. At the time, there was still no divorce in Ireland, so it had to be a legal separation. The process was long, arduous and expensive.

I couldn't stop thinking about the injustice of it all, how my supposedly 'significant other' had dedicated his life's work to making mine a merciless avalanche of misery. The marriage had been a disaster from day one. It was tantamount to living a recurring nightmare. Kieran, my husband, had come into the marriage with enough extra baggage to fill a conveyor belt in Heathrow. Sixteen years later, recounting his verbal and physical violence still disturbs me greatly. He had an uncontrollable temper, which was exacerbated by drink and drug binges. The violence had started with a little push or shove. Gradually it intensified into slaps, kicks and thumps. Once I had been held down on the stairs and almost strangled. The gold chain I had worn around my neck had cut into my throat, leaving a hideous red mark in its wake. My legs had angry raised welts left by boot-marks. Bruised cheeks and black eyes were commonplace. Kieran was verbally, physically and mentally abusive to me in public as well as in private. I had been subject to all kinds of name-calling, such as 'whore', 'slut' and, his favourite, 'mental patient'. The phrases varied but were always degrading and defamatory.

I was often deprived of money in a vain attempt to obstruct me from telling the outside world about my distress. I became a prisoner in my own home. I had been pissed on in bed, had bottles of wine poured over me, and been savagely kicked around my front garden in full view of the neighbours.

I finally packed my bags when Kieran punched my five-year-old son in the mouth so badly that he dislodged his front tooth and it cut right up into his gum. I temporarily moved into a friend's house while I was waiting for a barring-order hearing in court. Kieran was still using every opportunity available to him to make the simplest things difficult. He refused to pay child support, deliberately messed up access visits, and used these visits to hurl more abuse at me. My husband circulated malignant tales about me to anyone who was bored enough to lend a willing ear. He stalked my neighbours' houses, my friends and family, writing letters and making silent phone calls. The attacks were vicious and relentless.

Eventually I procured a barring order and was able to move back home. I was still terrified that the attacks would continue. I was right. The police service had to be called on fourteen different occasions. He tried to break into the house (succeeding on one occasion, and beating me senseless) and had to be handcuffed and dragged out, for all and sundry to witness. The children were petrified and crying, and I had to install an alarm, Chubb locks and bolts on all points of entry to the house. I had procured umpteen protection orders and barring orders. These turned out to be useless bits of paper: every time the police arrived, he had been and gone. The police kept telling me that they had to catch him in the act. All bullies are by nature cowards, so by the time the police did turn up, the damage was often well done, and the pathetic, spineless thug had long since absconded. It was so frustrating. Even the court orders, coupled with the efforts of the Gardaí, failed to protect me and my children.

The children and I lived in perpetual fear, both in the house and out in public. We were never free from the threat of the next attack. For twelve long months, the harassment continued. Looking back, I have no idea how I managed to stay sober through it all.

Charlie sat opposite me, dressed in a chequered waistcoat, grey flannel slacks, rust-coloured cowboy boots and a heavy woollen black overcoat that smelled distinctly of April rain. He was emptying sugar sachets into his coffee. One packet, two packets, three. He did this all the time, his head tipped down, saying very little to start with.

Stir, stir, stir.

The poor creature had come to realise that when we rendez-voused, he hadn't a snowball's chance in hell of getting a word in for at least half an hour. I bamboozled him with a detailed retelling of the day's stresses and strains. I gave him elongated accounts of what it really felt like being in 'the depths of recovery'. He swirled his spoon slowly around his cup, staring intently into it, as if it contained a view of the Grand Canyon.

'Are you listening?'

'Yep.'

'I can't sleep.'

'Yep.'

'No one cares.'

'Uh huh.'

'When I do sleep, I have these mad dreams. The dream I had last night was so long – in technicolor too. There was this old man, right? This old man, and he started talking to me. His mouth was moving and words were coming out, but I couldn't understand them, and I said "Get away, I don't know you."'

'Uh huh.'

'"Yes you do", he says. "Yes you do, yes you do." Three times, just like I said there. Then suddenly I was on a wave, surfing in Thailand, and a funny little woman gave me a bowl of porridge, only the porridge wasn't porridge, it was cat food, and not the good stuff, like Whiskas – you know, the cheap stuff you get in Crazy Prices.'

'Mmmm.'

'And then I was flying across the rooftops with a hammer in my hand, and noticed I had these strange wings coming out of me arse. Then I was falling down a big black hole, and Tom Jones passed me, and he was eating a Crunchie, and then I woke up.'

'Humph.'

'Well?'

'Well what?'

'What does it mean?'

'It means you had a dream.'

'Oh, fuck you.'

'Humph.'

'I wander around the house all night talking to myself. Do you think anyone notices? The kids don't even wake up. My family never call me. I'm so alone.'

'Mmmm.'

'I'm doing my best. I'm not drinking.'

'Good.'

'I'm going to my meetings. I'm doing all the right things.'

'Uh huh.'

'I'll probably rot up there in the house. When the smell gets bad enough, the neighbours will call Dyno-rod.'

'Mmmm.'

'Not because I'm dead. Only because the smell is so fucking horrendous. Then they'll come knocking for my contribution to the Dyno-rod bill, miserable bastards.'

'Uh huh.' Swirl, swirl, swirl.

'You're not listening to me.'

'I *am* listening.'

'No one listens; no one understands.'

Charlie yawned. A lengthy, exaggerated yawn.

'And that fucking bastard! I haven't a penny to my name. While he's out getting pissed and doing drugs, the children have no clothes. I need money for their schooling. He doesn't give a rat's arse; I can't get a penny out of him. I barely have enough food to get us through the week. He rang the house phone twenty-two times yesterday. I had to take it off the hook. He won't leave us alone. I had to call the police again too. We're on first-name terms now, me and the cops. We're friends. Welcome to the sad bastards' club. My only friends are the cops. Sometimes they call in when I haven't even put in a 999 – you know, for a little chat. I know how many sugars they take in their tea, for fuck's sake.'

'Mmmm.'

'What in God's name was I thinking when I got married?'

'You can't always be happy. You have to get married some-time. Look at me. I was married for twenty years. You wouldn't get that for murder.'

'I swear to Christ I can't wait to get him into court. I'll wipe the floor with him.'

Charlie propped his chin in his left hand and leaned his elbow on the table.

Swirl, swirl, swirl.

'Will you stop swirling that fucking spoon before I end up sticking it in your eye?'

He stopped.

'And his stupid solicitor's letters. When I wake up and go downstairs and see another one on the floor, my whole body starts to shake. I walk around with the letter in my hand, terrified to open it, all the time wobbling all over like some giant slab of Chivers jelly.'

'Can I give you a tip about those solicitor's letters? Never *ever* open your mail, without first having your breakfast, a cup of tea and a fag.'

'That's fucking ingenious, Charlie.'

'It works.'

'I paced all night, planning my opening statement. I'll tear the arse out of him. I resent hugely that I have to pay him money to buy my own house.'

Charlie looked up. 'It's only PFO money.'

'What's that?'

'Please Fuck Off money. What price for peace of mind? You'll be well rid of him.'

'I have my opening statement all worked out.'

'Your opening statement?'

'Yeah. It's brilliant. I wrote it all down. Want to read it?'

He coughed loudly, covering his mouth with his hand, a

smirk on his face, his blue eyes twinkling with wisdom.

'What you laughing at?'

'Ah. The midnight court syndrome – I hate the bastards.'

'Huh?'

'"He said, I said, he said, I said"? Do you really think the judge is going to read all that shite on the day? They don't even glance at the affidavits. The whole thing is about money, that's all.'

'I hate his guts.'

'Tell me this. When you were pacing the bedroom plotting revenge, was he in the room with you?'

'What?'

'Was he in the room with you? Was he in the house?'

'What are you talking about, you gobshite. Of course he wasn't in the room!'

'How long is it since he's been in the house?'

'I don't know . . . a good few months at least.'

'So you're pacing all night talking to someone you haven't seen in months.'

'Well I . . . .'

'Do you know what resentment is, Cathy?'

'Yeah. It's wanting to hire a hit man. Do you know any? You have a few hard men living over in your area. They must know some paid assassins.'

'Resentment is you taking the poison and expecting the other person to drop dead.'

'I would still take the poison.'

'Cathy . . . .'

'How much do you reckon a hit man would cost? I mean, I don't exactly want to murder him . . . that would be hard on the kids. A knee-capping might be cheaper, or maybe just an old-fashioned hiding. Just kick the fucking head off him.'

'You're not listening.'

'OK, I've got it: a gun to the head. Take him down a beach somewhere, get someone to put a gun to his head. That would work, wouldn't it? Jesus, there'd be some smell in the car after, but . . . .'

'Cathy?'

'What?'

'Who are you really fighting?'

I looked up at him.

'Can't you see? He's not there any more. He's not in your life. Disregarding the annoying telephone calls, while you're ranting and raving at the bedroom walls, take a look around you. Is he actually there? No, he ain't. So the next time you're pacing the floor indulging in the midnight courts, unable to sleep and feeling sick to your stomach, will you try to remember that he's probably fast asleep, in his bed, in his flat, snoring his fucking head off.'

'I know, I know.'

'But you *don't* know. That's your problem. You have to learn that you don't know.'

'I *do* know. I know for sure I hate the bastard's fucking guts, and if there was a way to resurrect the bubonic plague, I would send it to him in the post. No, wait! Was the Black Death more agonising, or the same thing as the bubonic plague? No, I've got it: leprosy. Imagine walking around Tesco's and you find your arm in the trolley at the checkout. Jesus, that must hurt.'

'Let go – let God. You do know what that means? You let go of the outcome. God will take care of that. You'll have your day in court, and justice will prevail. You can't take matters into your own hands. This resentment will kill you before it kills him. If you want revenge, you'd better start digging two graves, one for you and one for him. Can I make a suggestion?'

I shrugged. 'I really can't stand this any longer.'

'When you can't stand it any longer, try kneeling. Start praying for him.'

'Are you for fucking real?'

'Start praying for him.'

'You're having a laugh.'

'You have to start praying for him. Your resentment

will leave when you do. Give it a couple of weeks.'

'I can't pray for him. I can't!'

'You must, or you won't stay sober.'

'OK, I'll pray for him. May he have an eternal, excruciatingly painful death, amen.'

'That's not quite what I meant.'

'How can I pray for him? I can't even remember the Hail Mary – or the Our Father, for that matter.'

'You know the best prayer ever?'

I delayed my response, basically because I didn't have one.

'It's simple. Just say "God help me".'

'God help me?'

'Yes. God help me. Brilliant, isn't it?'

'Charlie?'

'You get on your knees and you pray for him.'

'And say what, exactly? How can I say anything nice about him when I hate him? He's a complete bollox.'

'You get down on your knees and you say, "Dear God, please help that bollox."'

'I can't believe what I'm hearing. I'm suffering here, and you're telling me to pray for that bastard . . . .'

'You want to be free of that anger? You want a decent night's sleep?'

I had run out of words.

'Go home. Get on your knees. Pray for him. Do it every night for a couple of weeks. Your resentment will be gone. It works, trust me. I don't know a lot, but I do know this: you'll be OK, no matter what.'

I went home.

Begrudgingly I got down on my knees, and said out loud: 'Dear God. Please help that bollox.'

My son Jason walked into the room at the same time. Reece, my daughter, came flying in behind him in her walker.

'She's been drinking again,' Jason explained to his little sister. She nodded and sucked her soother.

I cursed the day I ever walked into Alcoholics Anonymous.

Two weeks later, Charlie said 'Well?'

'Well what?'

'Did you do what I told you?'

'What are you on about?'

'You know what I'm on about. Did you do what I suggested?'

I was rightly pissed off. I thought I had got away with it. The praying thing hadn't been broached at all since that night in the coffee shop. This "leave well enough alone till the shit hits the fan" tactic was to become a frequent one with Charlie. He always waited for his moment.

'Yes, I did what you suggested.'

'Is it working?'

'Obviously not. I still hate the bastard.'

Snigger, snigger.

'It's not funny. I got another affidavit in the post today. It goes on forever. It could be a novel. I'm not drinking, so why isn't the God thing working? Why isn't He helping me out?'

'You're not sober through your own efforts . . . . When will you learn that? If anything has you sober, it's the God in your life.'

'This God thing you keep banging on about. He keeps moving the goalposts.'

'Maybe you're just crap at taking penalties.'

'Look, this praying lark doesn't work.'

'How are you so sure? You haven't even really tried it properly.'

How did he know I had given up after the first night?

'You said two weeks.'

'I said a couple.'

'A couple . . . that's the same thing. If it's not two weeks, then you need to tell me how long this takes.'

What a pathetic creature I was. My co-dependency was so acute, I almost needed to phone Charlie to ask him whether or not I should open up a carton of yoghurt.

'Get on your knees again. Start praying for your former husband, requesting everything that you would want for yourself.'

'I can't do this.'

'Trust me. It works. Give it some more time. You have to practise, practise, practise. What are the things you most want in your life?'

'Money, success, good health.'

'Go on.'

'Emm. Laughter, freedom from addiction, peace of mind, good sleep, a loving partner.'

'Now you're getting there.'

'No, I'm not. I want those things for *me*. Even if I do pray that he gets them, I won't mean a word of it.'

'That doesn't matter. Pray that he gets everything he could possibly want from life; you may even get some of the same things yourself.'

'That's highly unlikely. It's blood that runs through my veins, not holy water.'

'Do as I say, you rotten rip.'

'I hate your guts!'

'I love you too.'

I went back home and started again. This time, I really tried to concentrate while I prayed, despite the seething hatred that was still corroding my thoughts. I got on my knees and closed my eyes tight. I tried to think of all the wonderful things I wanted for myself, and I asked God to give them all to Kieran instead. I asked that he would always know peace of mind, that he would meet the love of his life, and that they would enjoy fantastically satisfactory sex. I asked that he would find a suitable, well-paid and interesting job; that he would have good health; that his fridge would always be full of the best food; that he would find laughter and fun. That he would find freedom from all addictions. That he would win the Lotto twice over. I asked that he would find loyalty, affection and kindness; that he would get to travel the world. I even prayed that he would learn how to be a good father.

I rang Charlie about two weeks later.

'Something weird happened today.'

'Uh huh?'

'I stopped using the word "bollox".'

He laughed out loud.

'I actually said his name. It happened by accident.'

'Ah.'

'What does that mean?'

'It means it's working.'

'I still hate him.'

'Did I say at any stage that you would stop hating him?'

'No.'

Pause.

'Will I?' I asked, beginning to crack. I truly did not want to be in a constant state of abhorrence, ricocheting through life with nothing but hostile thoughts and ill-feeling towards my ex-husband.

'I used to know this guy from meetings. Actually, I didn't really know the man at all, but I hated him. I remember I went to my sponsor one day, because it was really bothering me. I said: "Hey, why do I hate this man? I don't even know him, but I instinctively hate him." My sponsor said: "Go over and talk to him. Say hello. Introduce yourself." I said: "You must be joking."

'So I go over to this guy and I put out my hand and I say "Hello. My name is Charlie. What's yours?" And the man says his name and he starts talking about this and that, and I'm not really listening to him because it's suddenly dawning on me why I hate him so much.'

'Yeah?'

'He's me.'

'Huh?'

'He's me. In the flesh. Moody, egotistical, cynical. A carbon copy of me. No wonder I hated him so much. It wasn't his fault he was like me. He hadn't deliberately set out to mirror back to me my own horrible self, the one thing I detested more than anything else in this life.'

The penny is dropping.

'I stopped hating him there and then. In fact, we became quite good friends. He's dead now, God rest him.'

I go very, very quiet.

'Keep praying,' Charlie says, and hangs up.

I kept praying, and the most extraordinary things began to take place. I found that, unconsciously, a vague sincerity had begun to seep into those prayers. The words felt and sounded different. Out of nowhere, the seed of compassion was born. I was developing an authentic desire for my former husband to be happy. It didn't happen overnight, but it did happen. The more I prayed, the more earnest became the words I uttered. I found, after repeated efforts, that I fervently wanted him to have peace, a good life, some happiness. The hatred was soon replaced by a benign benevolence. Of course, I would be lying to myself and you if I were to claim that my incumbent hatred was obliterated. It wasn't. But I knew moments, even hours, when I was free from the obsession, and those spells grew longer and longer.

I soon began to add other people to my 'wish list'. If it worked with Kieran, why shouldn't it work with others? As you can imagine, the list grew extensively. I began to hog those little praying stations in churches. I had so many candles to light, no one else could get a penny in edgeways. Always a sucker for detail, I had to retire to bed earlier just to get through the endless catalogue of names.

Some weeks later, Charlie and I were chugging along in the 'Brown Rat' down the main Finglas Road, on our way to a meeting.

'Guess what?' I said.

Charlie was wearing a very old mauve-coloured sheepskin coat, the collar wound tightly around his neck with a purple and yellow scarf, embellished with a secondary-school crest. On his feet were a pair of light-up Nike trainers, scuffed and muddy, with unmatching laces, one white, one brown.

'I got the court date,' I said.

'When is it?'

'Next Tuesday,' I said, trying to sound unruffled.

'Do the right thing, and the right thing will happen. You're four months sober. If you tell the judge the truth, you'll come out tops. I know you'll be OK.'

'Can I not bend the truth a little?'

'You can, of course, but you'll pay the price.'

I sighed.

'You sleeping?' Charlie asked.

'Like a log.'

'Isn't that something? Nothing like a really good night's sleep. Peace of mind . . . you just can't buy it.'

'No, you can't.'

'When the judge speaks to you, look him directly in the eye. When you're challenged, bite your tongue.'

'Yeah, yeah.'

'No. Do it! Bite your tongue. Like this.'

He turned to me, stuck out his tongue, and bit it.

I did.

'That hurts!'

'Exactly.'

'I'm scared,' I said, tears welling up.

'So, you keep doing as I say. Say the Serenity Prayer before you go into court. Say it a hundred times if you have to. Actually, say it right now. Out loud.'

'God grant me the serenity to accept the things I cannot change, the courage to change the things I can, and the wisdom to know the difference.'

'I was just checking to see that you do actually know it.'

'What if prayers don't work? I'm afraid of Kieran.'

'If ever I feel threatened by someone, I imagine them sitting on a toilet doing a great big shite.'

I imagined my ex sitting on the jacks, and I started to

laugh and cry at the same time.

'I promise you this: if you are honest, nothing will go wrong.'

At that very moment, the car skidded to a halt at a traffic light. The battery had failed.

'You sure about that?' I asked, as the rain poured through the broken windows.

When the court date arrived, I was a gibbering wreck. I paced outside the building, maniacally sucking the guts out of cigarettes. As soon as I had finished one, I lit another. If I could have juggled ten in my mouth simultaneously, I would have. I babbled an emphatic liturgy of loud and lengthy meditations ('I am loved. I am lovable. There is nothing to fear. I am already a success'), stopping only briefly to do my lizard impression (sticking my tongue out and biting it).

My solicitor indicated that it was time to go inside. I stabbed out my half-finished ciggy, muttered a few more affirmations ('I am a powerful, loving human being. I am a child of the universe') and blessed myself three times in succession.

Out of the corner of my eye, I observed the tail-end of the Brown Rat, parked across the road, illegally. Charlie was sitting inside reading a newspaper. He waved at me, then stuck out his tongue and bit it.

The sight of him was a spirit-lifter. I waved back frantically, extending my tongue, biting it and pointing to it with my forefinger. I was so touched that Charlie had come, and felt reassured by his presence. The court hearing was in camera, so Charlie couldn't come inside, but just knowing that he was there comforted me. The knowledge that I was not alone made me calm and clear-headed.

'Everything will be OK. I know you'll be OK,' I heard him say in my head.

I knew too that I would be all right, no matter what happened inside the legal chambers. Someone had thought enough of me to drive into town, park illegally and wait outside the court to support me.

I stood before the judge, confident and relaxed.

I told him my story, and I won.

I have been in court several times since over marital and maintenance matters, and I have achieved successful outcomes. On every occasion, I imagined Charlie standing next to me, telling me: 'Everything will be OK. I know you'll be OK.'

And I always have been.

3

By the time I was six months sober, life had improved considerably. I continued to go to nightly meetings with Charlie, catching local AA sessions during the day alone. On Saturdays, my former husband took the children, so, to keep myself occupied, I went with Charlie to car boot sales. To my surprise, I caught the bug. Having no regular income, and two children to support, I began to bring my own bits and bobs to sell.

I have very fond recollections of those frivolous afternoons. Some days we made twenty pence, on other days twenty pounds. Whatever we earned, we split down the middle. The distraction provided a fleeting, yet much-deserved, escape from the more sombre enterprise of abstemious living.

Despite the fact that my junk was of a higher calibre than

Charlie's, he always seemed to make more sales than me. To this day, I cannot pinpoint why. I would watch him lay out his 'antiques' on a large, grey, hairy blanket, and be stupefied when people exchanged money for a cracked toilet seat, or a plastic, headless doll. We seemed to break even, nearly always earning about enough for a pouch of tobacco and a few coffees. These blessings were deeply gratifying. I found a sense of reward and fulfilment in the mundane and trivial. Simplicity, its application to daily living, and the resulting serenity, were things I began to appreciate and nurture. I tried to keep everything as straightforward as possible. The less I complicated my life, the more peace I gained. Ordinariness had become a staunch ally in the fight against self.

I was sleeping well. I was eating properly, making sure to have three square meals a day. I put on a little weight, and a certain flush had been rekindled in my usually fair-toned face. The kids were doing well. My six-year-old son's performance in school improved, and he did his homework every day. I caught up with most household chores, even adding a few home improvements. I was still plagued by financial insecurity. Charlie took me to the post office and told me to pay five pounds off my bills each week. If I did that, he said, I would have no letters or calls from debt collectors. It was a simple resolution, and it worked.

Charlie continuously told me that 'a grateful alcoholic won't drink', and I accepted this. In the evenings, I got on my knees and thanked God for the smallest things. I listed them off one by one, and found to my surprise that I was actually grateful. I then began to record my blessings in a journal. Some days the notebook was overflowing. It might have been something as small as someone holding a door open for me, while I tried to push my daughter's buggy through; a smile from a neighbour; an extra packet of tobacco; the sun bursting through the clouds for an hour. Of course, I still had my off days. Unfortunately, it is part and parcel of the alcoholic's nature to cling to one bad day, immediately forgetting that the other six days were fine. When that emotional amnesia struck, I opened my journal and re-read my own handwritten accounts of hope. I was instantly made aware that there was always something to be grateful for.

Charlie suggested that I become the secretary at my anchor group of Alcoholics Anonymous. I did. Acting as secretary is highly recommended in early recovery. It is good for the alcoholic's humility, and encourages discipline. It entails setting up chairs, getting tea, coffee and biscuits for members, and making sure that the literature is readily available. Because the secretary does not participate actively during the meeting, it helped me to listen more carefully. I took my responsibility seriously, and this made me feel more a part of the group.

Charlie thought it only appropriate for me to celebrate my six months' sobriety in style. It was a harsh November evening. A biting north wind teamed up with showers of black sleet and glacial cold. Charlie wore an oversized, navy lumber-jacket, its collar upright and fastened tightly, concealing all but the intensity of his blue eyes. He wore thick woollen socks turned down over heavy, laced-up army boots. His hat of choice was silver grey, with a thin white satin rim. I had wrapped myself up in layer upon layer of old T-shirts, blouses and jumpers. I was wearing plenty of socks too, mismatched and of variable size. Couture and mindless trend-setting have never interested me in the slightest, so I didn't care what I looked like. We shivered and shook as we drove towards Rush. We found a cheap take-away along the seafront, our cold breath dissipating as soon as it hit the warm air inside. We slithered into our allotted seats, and Charlie ordered our food.

'Well, how you doing?' Charlie asked, rolling up a fag.

'Shite. I feel lonely a lot of the time. I mean, I *am* grateful – things have improved – but there's this guilty feeling, you know, about the kids, that I'm at meetings constantly, and not spending enough time with them. The anxiety is awful sometimes.'

'Humph.'

'I should be better than I actually am. I'm putting on weight too, which I detest – there's more of me to shower every day.'

'I've seen more weight on a butcher's knife.'

'I'm ten stone. I'm obese.'

'For Christ's sake, give over. You look like a knitting needle.'

'I feel so ugly. I look old all of a sudden, and everything is sagging. My tits are in Cork right now.'

'Then whoosh them up to Donegal.'

'I'm getting wrinkles too – not surprisingly, with all the stress. In fact, the only time the wrinkles come out of my face is when I open my bra.'

'Maybe you need a new one?'

'I can't afford it.'

'Oh, lighten up. If you learn to laugh at yourself, you'll be eternally amused.'

Charlie barked loudly into an old handkerchief and shifted his legs, a disgruntled scowl breaking out on his face.

'What's the matter with you?' I asked. 'You've a face on ya that could haunt a house. You did ask how I was feeling.'

'No, I did not. I asked you how you were doing, not how you feel.'

I let out a big sigh.

'Did you get the kids to school today?'

'Yes.'

'Did you make the dinner?'

'Yes.'

'Did you clean the house, do the shopping?'

'Yes, I did but . . . .'

'Did you ask God for help?'

'Yes but . . . .'

'Did you take alcohol today?'

'No.'

'Then shut the fuck up. You're doing well.'

I shut the fuck up.

The waitress came over with our orders.

'Is it meat or fish?' I asked miserably, stabbing at the food with my fork.

'Does it matter? It's dead.'

We tucked into our meagre fare, and before long we were blathering away.

'You know what really bugs me?' I said. 'These guys arriving at meetings in BMWs and Porsches and these monstrous four-wheel SUVs. Where do they think they are? This is Ireland, for Christ's sake, not the Australian outback.'

'Mmmm.'

'Living in their fancy mansions, taking two holidays a year . . . you know, one in the sun, the other skiing down Mount Everest.'

'Yup.'

'What's with the skiing thing anyway? Dressed in their

designer gear, ridiculously large sunglasses propped on their faces, cavorting up and down hills like giant Oompa-loompas. I don't get it. Apart from looking stupid beyond words, do these people have some kind of perverse death wish?'

'Uh huh.'

'Well, who am I to hold a grudge? Obviously they have so much money, they have run out of ideas about how to spend it. They clamber up and down hills with a pair of sticks and a monkey hat, recklessly mowing down trees and human beings. Then they have the effrontery to call it a "recreational sport". It's well for them being able to waste money on such rubbish. I haven't a fucking penny to my name, the kids are dressed by St Vincent de Paul, and the thing I call a washing machine is broken again: it makes sad little hiccoughing sounds when you press the "on" button.'

'Tut bleeding tut.'

'I'm tired of playing Orphan Annie and being poverty-stricken. It may be good for character-building, but let's be serious for a minute. Who the hell really gives a fuck if I'm as humble as a monk's boxer shorts?'

'Uh huh.'

'If I sneeze, it's £20.'

'Mmmm.'

'If I fart, it's another £50. And as for a family holiday, our vacations don't stretch further than the Costa del condom-littered, sewage-smelling Dollymount Strand.'

'Then get a job.'

'Excuse me, I can't even look up the situations-vacant column, because I can't afford to buy a newspaper.'

'You can call to the social welfare office, or FÁS. Even the local libraries display the daily newspapers; it's free, no excuses.'

'I can't get a job! I'm already run off my feet, with meetings and kids and the house . . . and I'm trying to get sober.'

'So the great Catherine Barry has decided to get sober, and the world owes you a living, right? Perhaps you think you should win the Lotto for your troubles. Well, welcome to the real world, pet. Time to wake up. Get a job. If you need more cash, you must earn it, and to earn it, you have to get back into the workplace. Where do you think other people get their money from . . . the fucking tooth fairy? They work for their luxuries, and they are entitled to them. Quit moaning and get a job. Idle hands make for the devil's work.'

I wasn't impressed. He kept on swirling his coffee, head dipped, the brim of his hat hiding a half-smile.

Much to my dismay, the following day Charlie arrived armed with newspapers, and the search for a part-time job was on. I had the mornings free from nine to one, but the chances of finding a job locally for which I was qualified were pretty slim. It felt like a doomed expedition. I was looking in a ginormous slurry pit for Willie Wonka's winning ticket. I kept on making excuses that I wasn't quite ready to take on such a big responsibility. Not because I was lazy, but because I was terrified at the thought of having to relate to other people. I had multiple commitments, and any additional stress might push me over the precipice I had created in my own mind – and on which I was permanently teetering.

Charlie knew I was riddled with fear and anxiety and that they were whittling away at my already low self-esteem. He wasn't letting me off the hook. He drove me around the neighbourhood, looking out for ads in shops and supermarkets, helping me register with employment agencies and combing through the noticeboards in FÁS offices. He sat with me while I etched out a polished and upbeat curriculum vitae. The completed document was reasonably impressive. I had even surprised myself. Charlie made use of all his contacts, informing friends and business associates that I was looking for work. There was no escape from his dogged insistence that I get a job.

'Trust in God. It will come. The perfect job will land in your lap. Wait and see. Whatever happens, I know you'll be OK.'

The fact that Charlie was so reassuring encouraged me, and I sent my CV to over fifty local employers, and waited.

Two weeks later, I got a phone call from a local post office asking me to attend for an informal chat. On the day, I made myself look lady-like and professional. I had borrowed a functional two-piece suit from a friend, and had shoes and a bag to match. Off I tottered in my patent black one-inch high heels, trying to look as clerical and 'Ugly Betty' as possible. Charlie waited outside. Just knowing he was there calmed me. Before I went inside, I blessed myself and said the Serenity Prayer, and when I sat down for the interview a feeling of peace washed over me, just as it had in the courtroom.

I did a really good interview, and two days later came the call that I had the job, as a part-time cashier. I started the following Monday. Charlie was outside my front door and he drove me to work. He was there every day at 8.30 am, bolstering my self-esteem with pep talks.

'You can do for four hours what might appal you to have to do for the rest of your life,' he said. 'One day at a time. You can do it.'

When I finished at one o'clock, Charlie would be outside waiting to take me home. The day I held my first pay cheque, I cried. I treated the kids to some good sirloin steak. As we tucked into our well-earned mini-feast, I saw peace and joy around our kitchen table. The kids were smiling, and so was I. I had never felt so proud.

About six weeks into my new job, disaster struck. I was sent to the storeroom to retrieve some stationery that we had run out of at the front desk: pens, paperclips, staples, coloured folders, display pockets, lever arch files, and reams of blank paper. Before I knew it, I had taken some paper clips, staples and paper and shoved them into my briefcase. I rationalised that no one would miss them. I didn't tell a soul about my theft, but I knew such behaviour was dishonest.

I was still attending my meetings and acting as secretary but, before long, I began to fall off the AA beam. A restless uneasiness had set in. My conscience, now finely tuned to the truth and nothing but the truth, ranted at me. The pesky running commentary played over and over in my head. I could no longer claim the moral stance of someone who knew no better. I could not claim that I did not know what I was doing. The sad fact was that I *did* know better.

Much to my dismay, it became apparent that once you truly learn something, you cannot conveniently 'unlearn' it. I was well and truly snookered. I began to find it difficult to concentrate on the most minute task. Disturbing dreams roused me from my sleep. Still, I kept the dirty secret to myself. I was unable to confide in anyone because of the truckload of shame I was carrying inside. I tried to wrestle with my conscience. Why had I stolen some stationery when I knew I could afford to buy it? It made no sense. As the weeks passed, my ignominy trebled, then quadrupled, until it became like an open festering scab I kept picking at.

Before long, the wretched indiscretion had begun to wreak havoc on my daily chores. I became exasperated and enraged at the slightest thing. I found myself yelling at the kids over domestic trivialities. At work, I was unable to maintain any kind of equilibrium. It wasn't long before unwarranted and mind-blowingly inane errors began to appear in my work. I became withdrawn and sullen. I stopped sharing in AA meetings, and was broody and silent with Charlie. He never asked me what was wrong; he left me to figure it out for myself. It wasn't that I didn't trust him enough to tell him; it was the horrible shame about my own behaviour that stood between us like the Berlin Wall. I couldn't tell him because I was certain that he would reject me, and I could not bear the thought of that.

Charlie, being Charlie, just waited.

Six weeks after I had filched the items, I had an overwhelming urge to get drunk. The intensity of the unexpected return of the cravings was terrifying. I had been almost eight months sober, and Christmas was approaching. Alcohol seemed to have encircled me. I felt its malevolent presence all around me, and could not escape. In my twisted opinion, the entire nation, bar me, was contentedly pissed. Christmas parties were two a penny, and there was standing room only in the pubs. If I turned on the television, I was assaulted by ad after ad for this drink or that drink. When I went shopping, I noticed people loading up their trolleys with crates of beer and boxes of wine. I felt like Alice in Wonderland being tempted to succumb to its evil chant: 'Eat me, drink me, eat me, drink me!'

I had not been vigilant enough to spot alcohol's insidious lies worming their way back into my thinking. That is the nature of the beast. It doesn't walk in and announce itself; it makes itself at home long before anyone even suspects that it's a lodger. It shrouds itself in an invisible skin. Its persistent goading had become a daily occurrence, and it followed me around like a little devil on my shoulder. 'Go on, have one drink. One drink won't do any harm. Sure, it's Christmas. Everybody has a drink at Christmas. Have one. No one will know anything about it. You can start being sober again after you've had a few drinks. You did it before; you can do it again.'

The craving for booze was a shock to my system. I had been sober long enough to appreciate what a good life I could have if I stayed off the jar. I was out of debt, and the kids were coming along fine. I had plenty to lose. The greatest thing sobriety had given me was peace of mind: moments of clarity and serenity. These were gifts I knew money could not buy. I was panic-stricken at the prospect of losing it all. On Christmas Day, Charlie called in and gave me a card, which read: 'To Charlie, from Peggy, Christmas 1992.' He had crossed out that bit with a green felt marker and written under it: 'To Cathy, from The Hat, Christmas 1993.' As an afterthought, he had footnoted: 'What the hell . . . they're a bleeding waste of money anyway.'

On St Stephen's Day, my former husband had the kids. Charlie suggested that we drive to St Ita's Psychiatric Hospital in Portrane to attend an AA meeting. I had never seen a psychiatric hospital before, let alone been inside one. As we hurtled up the long driveway, we were confronted by a dark, foreboding Victorian-style building. The windows were barred from top to bottom. It loomed before us like something out of *The Amityville Horror* movie.

'Why did we have to come here?' I moaned. 'It's so depressing. Can't we go to another meeting somewhere else?'

'No, not tonight.'

We got out of the car. Charlie was unusually quiet, but purposeful, as he ushered me through the front door.

Once I was inside the building, the smell hit my nostrils immediately: a mixture of urine and disinfectant, and something else that was all too familiar: the stench of loneliness and abandonment was all-encompassing. Patients with gaunt, vacant faces shuffled along in their pyjamas and nightgowns, the swish-swish of their slippers dragging across the tiled floor. They moved aimlessly, their bodies animated, their souls all but deceased. I remember noticing how young they were. It was a shocking revelation.

I turned to Charlie and he instinctively knew what I was thinking.

'I know,' he said, slipping his arm into mine and guiding me down one of the many corridors. 'They are younger than you. So sad.'

I wanted to leave there and then, but instead found myself gliding along on Charlie's comforting arm, all the while coming face to face with the devastating consequences of mental illness. The sickly smell of delusion: the forlorn, sedated eyes of people who had left the earthly plane, stigmatised and scorned by an uncaring society. Worse again, the grieving faces of their loved ones, those forced to stay behind, within the boundaries of reality. The clinical and poker-faced nursing staff, grown immune to the anguish, the mental suffering.

We passed through wards, and I saw the sparse metal-framed beds circumscribed by tawdry floral plastic curtains. The wild stares of some patients caught my eye. Others meandered up and down, mumbling incoherently.

A young man, no more than twenty years old, raced up to me and gripped my arms.

'Have you a cigarette please?' he implored.

I froze.

Charlie reached into his pocket and handed him a pre-rolled cigarette.

'Thank you,' the young lad said, lovingly rolling the cigarette between his fingers, sniffing at it repeatedly, as a dog would a bone.

I was close to tears, and angry at Charlie for forcing me into this hellhole. He must have sensed my disdain and kept a firm grip on my arm as we walked on. The domestic staff, the nurses, and even some of the patients nodded at him. Charlie pressed a buzzer, and a nurse unlocked a door.

She smiled at him, and said hello. Charlie remarked that it was brass monkey weather. She looked at me and nodded. Now it dawned on me what was happening. He was dumping me in a lock-up ward of a psychiatric hospital!

'I'm not going in,' I said, my voice cracking.

'Yes you are,' he said softly, and he pushed me gently through the door.

The poor devils incarcerated in this wing were all male, and they were all beyond help. They wandered around in torn and tattered nightclothes, oblivious to the excrement stains on their dressing gowns, staring blankly at walls.

'Why have you brought me here?' I asked Charlie angrily.

'Do you know what a wet brain is?'

'No. Do I need to?'

'See these men? They all have wet brains. It's a condition brought on by acute alcoholism – a condition from which there's no turning back. Alcohol has destroyed their brain cells. They have to be tube-fed. They wear nappies because they have no control over their bodily functions. Their brains are permanently damaged. They'll never know or be able to appreciate the simple things that you and I take for granted.'

'What has this got to do with me?'

'They're gone, Cathy. Finished. They may as well be dead. They'll never know the satisfaction of a good conversation. They'll never experience the joys of family life, the pure wonder of the innocent smile of a newborn baby. They'll never share the love of a spouse, relish the smell and taste of a bowl of home-made soup. They'll never feel the cool comfort of a swim in the ocean or the touch of the Mediterranean sun on their skin. They can't think, can't feel, can't sense, and can't function.'

I had begun to weep. I could hardly bring myself to look at the patients, the drool seeping down their chins, the smell of shit and piss that permeated the air, the limp carcasses that were once walking, talking, vibrant human beings, now lying there, waiting to die.

'You seen enough?' Charlie clenched my arm, so we were brought face to face.

'Yes,' I mumbled, unable to stop crying.

'Well, make sure you take one last long look. That's your future, if you want it.'

'I don't want it. I don't want to end up like that.'

'Well, you'd better start telling me what's bothering you then, because you've been doing a hell of a lot of talking, but saying nothing.'

I put my head down.

'If you don't tell me what's on your mind, you'll be drunk within the week.'

How did he know I was thinking of taking a drink?

'OK.'

He pulled me into his warm sheepskin coat and gave me a great big bear hug. 'Let's go get some coffee.'

In the coffee shop, I vomited up the truth. It came out in great big spews. I told him how I had stolen the stationery, and how I was confused as to why I had done it when I didn't have to. I told him of my shame. He listened without interrupting me, swirling his coffee, head dipped, holding his face in one hand, a roll-up hanging out of his mouth.

'The thing is, Charlie, I don't know why I did it. It's not like I haven't money for a few sheets of paper.'

He scratched behind his left ear.

'I jeopardised my job too.'

'Uh huh.'

'Then I had this overwhelming compulsion to drink the other day.'

'Humph.' Scratch, swirl, scratch, puff, puff.

'What the fuck is wrong with me anyway?'

'Can't stop touching the flame, can you?'

I shrugged.

'One of these days you'll get a nasty burn.'

'Christ, when will I ever learn?'

'Old habits die hard.'

'But I've been sober a good few months now. Why would I do such a thing, when I know better?'

'OK, let's put this whole thing in perspective. You didn't raid the post office, did you?'

'No, but I stole nevertheless.'

'Did you ever steal anything before this?'

I bowed my head.

'Yes. I did.'

'A lot?'

'Sort of.'

'What makes you think stopping drinking alone will change your behaviour? Stopping drinking is only the tip of the iceberg. The disease is what lies beneath, and the disease has great patience. While you think you are safe from it because you don't drink, it's doing sit-ups, quietly waiting for its chance to get you again. Alcoholism is a disease of the emotions. If you don't tackle the disease – those emotional disturbances that led you to destructive drinking in the first place – you will never stay sober.'

He drained the last of his coffee and ordered two more. I was chain-smoking now, and we sat in a cloud of our combined smog, while being pleasantly poisoned. We were like a couple of *Coronation Street* chimneypots.

'Change is hard work. It will not descend on you like some celestial donation.'

'You mean like being able to talk in tongues? I've met people who claim to be able to do that sort of thing, you know.'

'Emm, no, Cathy. That only happens to characters in the Bible.'

'Oh.'

'And crackpot maniacs who are institutionalised.'

'Right.'

'Us mere mortals have to settle for hard graft. Change means action. Change means persistent practice. You are trying to unravel thirty years of bad habits. If you walk thirty miles into a forest – which is a long way in – you must walk the thirty miles to get back out. You get my gist?'

I nodded.

'Sometimes our behaviour gets worse before it gets better. It's a bit like the instructions on the back of a medicine packet: "Please note that your condition may get temporarily worse before it improves." Did you ever hear the story about the guy who drowned in the canal?'

'No.'

'He rode into the canal on a bicycle and drowned. When they went to recover the body, they found he was still gripping the handlebars. Isn't it ironic that if he had let go of the handlebars, he might have lived? Being human, we tend to cling to what we know, even when it's the very thing that's going to kill us. And so it is with emotional sobriety. It involves hard, hard work. We all have defects of character, so character-building is a must. Me? I'm an exception to the rule, of course; more like a defect looking for a character.'

'The moral of the story being: if you see a burning bush, call the fire brigade.'

'I can still remember the day I first heard a lie popping out of my mouth. It was a revelation. Once that happens, you're fucked. You won't ever get away with anything again. It's called developing a conscience.'

'Tell me about it,' I said morosely.

'That's when you'll really begin to hate my guts and wish you had never heard of AA.'

'I fucking hear ya.'

'Good. For a moment there, I thought I saw distinct flames hovering above your head.'

'But how do I change my behaviour?'

'You know the story of Jack and the Beanstalk?' he asked, rolling a smoke.

'Yes. A couple of magic beans, a giant ogre and a twat who likes to climb trees and fall off them. Hey, can we get away from fiction for just one nano-second?'

'Jack opens the window and throws the beans out, right? And they grow into a beanstalk. Well, just remember that Jack and the Beanstalk *is a fairytale*!'

'No shit.'

'You can't throw seeds out the window and expect them to just take root and grow by themselves. You have to sow them, tenderly, carefully, so that they grow up good and strong when the spring comes.'

'So the Holy Ghost is, in fact, nothing more than a common gardener?'

'Did you hear anything I've just said?'

'Yes, but I just want to . . . .'

He put his hand to his mouth and made a 'zip it' gesture.

'You know, I once had a very good friend who got himself into a similar situation.' Charlie lit up and took a long, leisurely drag. 'A nice guy he was too. Young and stubborn of course, full of false pride, ego . . . kind of reminds me of someone . . . . He was doing great. Came to AA, got a sponsor, went to his meetings regularly and worked through the Twelve Steps. The family was healing, things improved at home and in his job; everything looked like it was plain sailing. Then he started doing secretary in AA. Three weeks into it, he went on a horrific bender that lasted for six months. By the time he got back into AA, his slip-up had damn near cost him everything. His job was gone, the family was torn apart, and his health was ruined. The usual story. He eventually confessed to his sponsor that he had started fiddling with the contribution bag. A pound here and there at first, then a fiver, and so on. No one knew what he was up to. You're as sick as your secrets – remember that, will you? You can't keep secrets.'

'I feel so ashamed,' I whispered.

'You know, that guy was a real howl. In his drinking days, he used to rob the poor boxes in the church. He always went for St Anthony first. There was a killing to be made on St Anthony.'

'Charlie, how do I make amends for what I've done? Should I put the stuff back?'

'St Jude was his second favourite: the patron saint of hopeless causes. The weight of the box alone would kill ya; you couldn't get money into it, never mind try to get some out.

Hopeless causes, eh? There's no fucking shortage of them in this country.'

'Charlie . . . .'

'Then one day he was so pissed, he got it into his head to climb the statue in the St Francis Xavier church and rob the jewelled crown off its head. Of course he fell, and a priest came and got him to a hospital, and in the hospital the guy in the bed beside him was an AA member, and he took him to a hospital AA meeting and, well, you can guess the rest.'

'Charlie, do I return what I stole?'

'You can't put the stuff back. What if you're caught and you lose your job? If I left my hat in a lions' den, would you think me crazy if I went back in to retrieve it?'

'Yeah, I suppose so.'

'How much do you put in the contribution bag when it goes around at the meeting?'

'What? I don't know. Any loose change I have – maybe fifty pence.'

'From now on, you put one pound in.'

'Right.'

'And if you ever have a few spare bob, go into a church and put it in the poor box.'

'Right.'

'Oh, and give St Jude a rest, or he'll be getting a big head.

There are other saints to be considered.'

And that's exactly what I did.

Fifteen years on in Alcoholics Anonymous, and I'm still doing it.

Not so long ago, I found myself actually sitting in the St Francis Xavier church on Gardiner Street. I was there to hear a gospel choir, having always wanted to sing in one. It was an experience I won't forget in a hurry. As I sat in the pew, I examined the church and the statues, and remembered Charlie's tale about his friend. It suddenly dawned on me that the 'friend' he had referred to just might have been himself.

4

I still kept finding soft places to fall. April rolled around, and with it came my first AA anniversary. A card arrived in the post from Charlie. I opened it and it said: 'Happy first birthday.' It had a big badge with the figure '1' on it. Inside the card he had sellotaped a blade of grass, and underneath that, a little story about how it had come from the Garden of Eden.

To this day, I have no idea what it was all supposed to mean. Suffice to say, it was very touching, and bore Charlie's character-istic trademark. Outside my front door, I found a tatty brown paper bag held together with a bunch of green staples. 'CATHY' was crookedly scrawled across it in block capitals, with a purple felt marker. I opened it, and inside was a kid's soft cuddly toy – a yellow chicken. He wore a green hat, a chequered lumberjack shirt and a pair of denim dungarees. When you squeezed his hand, he sang: "Old MacDonald had a farm, ee-iy-ee-iy-oh". Attached to the cuddly toy was a handwritten note informing me that the chicken had been christened 'Sob'. It went on to say that Sob would keep me company when I felt down in the dumps. He would listen to all my woes and never desert me, and that I was to cuddle up to him whenever I felt alone. I still have the card, and Sob. He has been with me through many a difficult time, and still sits comfortably on top of my computer, grinning down at me with his oversized, golden mandible.

I was beside myself, having finally reached the one-year-sober mark. I sat back confidently, waiting for the *other* cards to come. You know, from family and friends, and the job; perhaps a word or two from An Taoiseach or the President? At the very least, a short, profound acknowledgment from the Lord Mayor of Dublin. That not being feasible, a simple lowering of the flag to half-mast might have been an acceptable alternative.

However, the helium balloons, and grand-scale pyrotechnic displays failed to materialise. The DHL Express courier to whom I waved frantically for over fifteen minutes did not stop at my house laden down with alluring packages. My colossal ego was deeply wounded.

When I complained to Charlie about it, he said, deadpan:

'What do you want? A fucking minute's silence? Get over yourself.'

The size of my head shrank so fast, it could have been sold in the Philippines.

I had no reason to be carping. Bills were being paid, the grass was getting cut, my net curtains were washed, and the bin went out religiously every Tuesday evening. I was feeling better than I had done in ten years. Charlie kept turning up with his little gifts. An old kettle with no lead ('You can pick one of them up anywhere'), a watering can with holes in the bottom ('Some masking tape, and Bob's your uncle'), a shower curtain rail ('I know you've no shower, but you might have some day').

One evening, Charlie called to my house without warning. I was glad to see him. I had started to repaint the inside of the house, and had just about finished the front room. We made some tea, and sat on the settee admiring my work. I was hanging a few pictures back on the walls. Charlie got up and looked at one in particular. It was a poem which had been written on parchment paper in antique cursive writing style and set in a gold frame.

Charlie stood silently sipping his tea, reading the poem.

'God, that's brilliant,' he said.

'Yes. It was a wedding gift. I treasure it. It's very pretty, isn't it?'

'Yeah, it's very pretty, but forget that. I'm talking about the actual poem. It's bloody brilliant. Do you know who wrote it?'

'Yes. I did,' I said shyly.

He turned around to face me.

'Are you having me on?'

'No.'

'You wrote that?'

'Uh huh.'

'No!'

'I've been writing since I was a kid.'

'You never told me you wrote.' He was clearly surprised.

'You never asked.'

'Have you ever considered submitting this for publication?'

'Are you jesting? It's rubbish. I only hung it up there because it looks pretty.'

'Take it down. It's too good to be hanging on a wall. You should send it to a poetry publisher immediately.'

'Don't be stupid; no one's going to read any of my poems, let alone like them.'

'You mean there are others?'

'Yes, lots. In a drawer upstairs.'

'Well, what the fuck are they doing in a drawer? Have you ever submitted any of them?'

'No. Never! Like I said, I don't think they're any good.'

'I want to see them now.'

I went upstairs and retrieved the poems I had modestly penned over the years. Having never had the confidence to show them to anyone, I was hesitant about handing them over to Charlie. I fidgeted, polishing and tidying up while Charlie sifted through the endless reams of paper.

'Humph. Mmmm. Uh huh,' he muttered.

After what seemed like an age, he put the papers on the floor.

'I reckon it will take about five years,' he said rather prosaically.

'What?'

'I said I reckon it will take about five years.'

'Five years for what?'

'Five years before you're discovered. Miss Barry, you are one hell of a talented writer.'

'Have you been drinking? Let me smell your breath.'

'You know what? I never said this to anyone in my life, but I'm going to say it now. You're so good that I'm green with envy.'

I just stared at him.

At the time, I had a four-bedroomed house. One of the bedrooms had become a storage cum dumping room. Charlie offered to help turn it into something resembling an office space: a place where I could concentrate and write in peace. I thought it was an inspiring idea. We tidied it up as best we could, stacking items on top of each other to make more space. I had some paint left over in my back garden shed. Between the two of us, we had a fresh coat up in two hours. It made all the difference. We picked up a cheap desk and chair in a second-hand furniture shop. I used a sheet from the hot press as a table-cloth, placed the broken typewriter on top, and it was move over Shakespeare – here I come!

Charlie told me to type out the poems. He bought me *The Writers' & Artists' Yearbook*, a kind of writers' bible. I referred to it often for tips and contacts. Charlie also taught me how to submit my work. The poem that had been hanging on the wall was the first I ever submitted, and the first I ever had published. It was so exciting: I remember leaping around the hall with the magazine in my hand. When I showed Charlie, he beamed with pride. I began to submit my work regularly.

I had as many rejections as acceptances. In fact, I had so many rejection slips at one stage that Charlie suggested we wall-paper the room with them. A stamped addressed envelope always went out with my work, and I kept a record of everything. It wasn't long before I had about ten poems published. At that stage, Charlie had begun to coach me on short-story writing – something he did himself. I baulked at the idea initially, insisting that I had neither the necessary talent nor the commitment. My feeble objections were overruled. Soon, Charlie had me writing short stories. He gave me ludicrous themes to work with, such as 'Write about a one-legged blind waitress' or 'A bomb that explodes in a restaurant on St Valentine's Day.' Despite my protestations, I always managed to create some kind of narrative.

Pretty soon, my short stories began to appear in newspapers and women's magazines. My passion for writing had returned tenfold. I wrote every day. My fervour for reading also returned. I had been an avid reader when I was younger, but alcohol had robbed me of that simple pleasure.

I started going to the library again. Something about the ambience of the library brought me a great deal of tranquillity. The soothing silence, broken only by the whirr of the air conditioner, and the occasional delicate flutter of a page being turned. There was such simple pleasure to be gleaned from just being there.

While my son was in primary school and my daughter in Montessori class, I scribbled away. I brought each new piece to Charlie. His constructive criticism was always accurate. A little alteration here and there: add a line, omit another one, switch that paragraph around. He was always on the money. In return, I took his poetic endeavours and began to catalogue them. Charlie was a member of the two-finger-typist brigade and had to wear glasses most of the time. I enjoyed typing up his work and was only too willing to do it.

Saturdays and Sundays were the only days I got to lie in. A lie-in at the time consisted of a paltry thirty minutes max. My daughter was an early riser, and if I didn't get up with her, all hell could break loose – which it did one Saturday morning in May. The alarm had gone off but I had haphazardly flung my arm out from under the duvet and smacked the off button instead of the 'snooze' one. I was going to steal just another five minutes, and I rolled over.

When I awoke, it was 11 am. Jumping out of bed, I stopped dead in my tracks at the bedroom door, trying to figure out what the strange noise coming from downstairs was. Standing on the landing, I could hear water. Running water!

When I looked down the stairs, my daughter waved up at me with a big smile on her face. She was in her bathing suit, splashing around in about three inches of water.

'Jesus Christ!' I screamed, dashing downstairs, then wading through the water, which was flowing from room to room. The entire bottom half of the house was a lake. I splashed my way to the bathroom. All the bath and sink taps were on full. The bathroom sink was full of videos, and reams of black tape had clogged the plughole. The toilet was backed up with Parazone bottles, toothpaste and a toilet roll. A yellow rubber duck sailed past my feet, bobbing like a cork on the ocean. My daughter tugged at my soaking wet pyjama bottoms. I turned around and she held up a beach bucket in one hand and a spade in the other.

'Mammy play?' Reece said innocently.

I rang Charlie. To my disappointment, I got the answering machine. Charlie hadn't had an answering machine until then, and had always been one to detest newfangled gadgets.

'This is Charlie.' (Long pause, cough.) 'Eh. Ahem. Please leave your name and stuff on the thingamajig when it makes a funny noise. Humph. Cough. Humph.' Bleeeeeep . . . .

'Where are you? I'm drowning!' I screeched.

While I waited for him to call back, I surveyed the damage. The carpets were destroyed, the walls watermarked. The couch and chairs were floating debris, and the lino in the kitchen had begun to bubble and peel away. I turned off the mains electricity and stood in the middle of it all, not knowing what to do. The phone rang. It was Charlie. I explained what had happened. Half an hour later Charlie was at the door, a bucket and mop in each hand. He came wearing a black two-piece suit, black tie and black hat, with a transparent plastic mac over the suit. On his feet he wore hideous, lime green wading boots.

'Are you coming out to play?' he asked.

I was not in the mood for his jokes. The spectacle at my front door of what appeared to be a funeral undertaker in large wellington boots failed to arouse a shred of jocularity in me.

I called my babysitter and asked her to take the kids out for a few hours while we tried to tackle the deluge. We started in the front room. Bucket by cumbersome bucket, we carried the water outside and ditched it onto the grass. It took three hours to get the water out. Charlie seemed to think the whole thing uproariously funny.

He whistled Frank Sinatra's 'My Funny Valentine' while we splish-sploshed through the leaking barge that had become my home. Now and then, he kicked up his lime green wellies, creating little breakers that slapped against the walls with a 'plop-plop-plop'.

'This is great gas, isn't it? I haven't had so much fun since me Mammy and Daddy used to take me to the beach.'

Splish, splosh, splish, splosh.

I was fit to be tied.

Admittedly, all my furniture had been hand-me-downs – second-hand items my family or good neighbours had donated – but it was the only furniture I had.

'I can't take this,' I wept. 'Everything is ruined. I can't afford to replace things. What the hell am I going to do now? I don't even have house insurance. Don't tell me. God will sort it. A fucking great big Arnotts truck full of furniture is on its way as we speak.'

'So now God is some kind of furniture warehouse manager?'

'OK, maybe Arnotts is asking a bit too much. I'll settle for Bargaintown.'

'Just who do you think God is: some kind of Ben Dunne of the heavenly realm?' he barked.

'Dunnes don't do furniture.'

'Neither does God.'

'Yes, odd that, isn't it? Jesus was a carpenter, was he not?'

Charlie threw me an exasperated glance.

'I do know you'll be OK.'

'Will you stop fucking telling me I'll be OK! I am sick of you giving me that pat answer. I will be OK. I will be OK. I *won't* be OK, right?' I screamed.

'Have I ever been wrong so far?' he asked calmly.

I flung the bucket across the room. It smashed against the wall.

'We needed that.' Charlie stroked his chin thoughtfully. He crossed the room, picked it up and studied it.

'It's broken,' he observed nonchalantly.

'Of course it's broken,' I yelled. 'Everything is broken. My life is broken. My house is broken! I mean, look at it. It's a fucking dump! Maybe it's OK for *you* to live in a shithole, but I don't particularly like it. I come from Clontarf, am educated, have good parents. I was going to be something. I shouldn't be here.

Stuck in this, in this . . . fucking . . . this fucking . . . .'

'Kip?'

I tripped over a Thomas the Tank Engine toy and went hurtling across the room, landing on the waterlogged couch, my legs sticking up in the air. Charlie stood, hands on hips, grinning from ear to ear. I swung around like some crazed rabies-ridden mongrel, glaring at him, challenging him to provoke me into active violence. I held the mop over my head, wielding it like a knife.

'You don't need to threaten me with that. You use words like artillery, Cathy. They're enough to wound anyone for life.'

That took the wind out of my sails. I stared at the mop in my hand. The old Cathy was back. I was back to my deplorable, obnoxious self. In my histrionics, I had insulted Charlie from a height. My vicious invective had hurt him deeply.

'Let go, let God,' he said quietly. 'Just. Let. Go. Trust in God. All this will be sorted.'

'And just exactly how am I supposed to let go? You keep telling me to let go, but no one on this earth seems to have a clue how to do it. I am sick of these clichés you keep throwing at me. I can't let go!' I screamed.

'Just shut the hell up and listen, for Christ's sake. Just listen, for once in your life, will you? It's so simple, but you have to make it so complicated. What you need to learn is to get stupid.

Get stupid!' he screamed right back at me, pointing his fingers at his brain, just in case mine had slipped out through my earlobes and somehow found its way into the bucket as well.

I went into shock. Charlie had never raised his voice to me. He pounded out of the room, breaking into a really bad coughing fit.

'Where's your telephone books?' he barked.

'What?'

'Where's your telephone directories?'

'On the table in the hall.' I wasn't going to incur his wrath a second time. He trudged back in, carrying the Golden Pages and two other big telephone books. Before I could say 'Last one in a straitjacket is a rotten egg', he thrust them into my arms.

'Hold them,' he said, 'and don't say another word for the next fifteen minutes.'

I wasn't sure if his face was puce from the coughing fit or from the outburst of temper. Maybe it was a bit of both.

Charlie filled buckets with water, disposing of them in the garden, sponged up the remainder, and then rung out the mop in the sink. When he'd done this, he repeated the process. He never so much as glanced in my direction or uttered a word. He whistled and sang as he went about his business – hopelessly out-of-tune Frank Sinatra songs.

I stood like a gobshite, clutching the books to my chest, not knowing whether to sit down or stand up. The singing was unbearable. Had my hands been free, and his throat within reaching distance, I would have performed an anaesthesia-free tonsillectomy.

'Those books hurting your arms yet?'

'No,' I lied.

Another five minutes passed. My arms had begun to ache.

'Heavy, aren't they?' he remarked as he walked in and out of the room.

I said nothing.

A kind of terminal silence had seeped in.

Another five minutes passed.

Charlie dried off his hands, staring at me.

'You OK?'

'Grand.'

My arms were fucking killing me. My shoulders ached from the strain, and my hands had turned white-knuckle numb. My neck felt stretched to pelican proportion.

'Sick and tired of holding those heavy books?'

'No.'

'Shoulders aching? Back sore?'

'Well, actually . . . .'

'Five more minutes,' he smiled.

I would gladly have done time for him right there and then.

My body had begun to shudder. I shifted from one foot to the other to try and balance the weight. When he came in five minutes later, I was buckled over like an old woman.

'Had enough?'

'I'm in agony.'

'Not easy carrying that weight, is it?'

'No.' I squeezed the word out through gritted teeth.

'What would make it better?'

'To drop them.'

'OK, let them go. Drop them with as much effort as you can muster.'

I let go of the telephone books, and they tumbled down, making a resounding splash. I let out a roar of blessed relief.

I shook out my hands, arched my back and rotated my neck, which was very tender.

'Feel better?'

'Do I fuck?'

'Cathy?'

'What?'

'That's how you let go.'

Two weeks later, the house still resembled the trenches of World War I. A solution didn't seem any nearer. I had thought about getting a Credit Union loan, or going to the bank, but I knew my income wouldn't stretch far enough to make the monthly repayments. Charlie had suggested that I pay a visit to the local community welfare officer and that I call the St Vincent de Paul. I hadn't much faith in finding Samaritan staff in the Department of Social Welfare. Nonetheless, I followed his practical advice and went.

I also put a call in to St Vincent de Paul, and representatives from the organisation came out to visit me. They were wonderfully understanding, and seemed genuinely interested in helping me out. Just talking to them made me feel less isolated. They brought clothes for the children and gave me some food vouchers, all of which were hugely appreciated. Still, it was carpets and furniture I needed the most. Some days after my visit to Social Welfare, I received a cheque, but it wouldn't have bought a wooden egg cup, let alone a chair or a couch.

So I found myself sitting on a minuscule, red plastic child's chair (a gift from Charlie's Emporium) in my unadorned front room, reading some AA literature and trying very hard to pray. In between the 'Our Father's and the 'Hail Mary's, the great post office robbery plan was being hatched. I had it all figured out, down to the last distressingly inadequate detail. I would get someone from the outside to hold me hostage, take all the money and then give me half of it back later. Simple, but brilliant.

Fuck the furniture. I would follow my dream of becoming a

writer. I would retire to a quaint cottage in Connemara and become immediately mute. I would wear hand-knitted shawls made out of crude sack and write only with ancient quills. I would invoke nature, walk along seashores, and be inspired to write profound and lengthy sonnets about the stark solitude of periwinkles. I would carry baskets of seaweed in from the tide, and do my best not to wince when a lobster became entangled in my wild, flowing chestnut locks. I would suffer for my art. Traipsing up and down Croagh Patrick silently and barefoot would be compulsory. So what if I had the clawed feet of a giant caribou? I would become rich and famous from my writing.

A commotion was going on outside. My front window was open, and street noise filtered through. Then there was an urgent knocking on the front door. I flung it open angrily.

A young woman in a parka jacket, a clipped folder and a mobile phone to her ear, stood on the doorstep. Charity, I assumed, or door-to-door sales people. I was sick and tired of the latter. I couldn't understand why they kept it up. It was obvious to anyone who had the intellect of a gnat that we were of meagre means. The grass was jungle-height. The only garden accessory was the overflowing, rodent-infested wheelie bin.

'Are you lot blind as well as thick?' I said, making to slam the door in her face. 'Maybe I should put a sign up in the garden? "Sorry. We can't help. Starved to death last week."'

'Listen, I'm not looking for money,' the woman said apologetically, trying to poke her head around the half-closed door.

I opened the door fully.

'That's what they all say. Whatever you're trying to peddle, I can't afford it. I'm busy making porridge for our dinner.'

'I'm Marie. I'm from Deadly Productions, the movie company. It's just that we're filming in the area, and we were wondering if we could use your house for lights and cameras, that sort of thing.'

'Is this some kind of a sick joke?'

'No.'

'Wait. I get it. Are you from the flats? You've got the wrong house, love. The crack cocaine dealer lives three doors down.'

'Do I look like a drug addict?' Her mobile phone was bleeping incessantly.

'Do I look like Bozo the Clown? Hey, what's going on out there?'

I stepped out onto the porch. The road was jammed with vehicles of all types. A rabble of strangers busied themselves with cranes, cable wires and camera tracks. The street was alive. All my neighbours had come out and were swarming the footpaths like armies of ants.

'What's the movie?' I asked.

'*The Van*. Roddy Doyle.'

'No way.' I was a big fan.

'Hey, you got any kids?' she asked as an afterthought.

'You offering to buy them? You can have them for free.'

'How many do you have?'

'Two, at the last count. Never trust a condom that glows in the dark.'

'We need extras. How old are yours?'

'One six, the other two.'

'We can use the six-year-old.'

'For what exactly? He's not much use, to be honest. Joined at the hip to his PlayStation.'

'He'll get paid well. Plus, we'll pay you for the use of your property.'

Property.

Someone had referred to my house as a 'property'.

And so it happened. *The Van* was filmed on set. We got paid £1,000: the exact amount I needed for carpets, lino and a suite of furniture. Brand new carpets and brand new furniture.

Charlie painted the walls with the little bit of money we had left over, and the house looked spanking new. What had originally presented itself as a complete disaster had turned out to be a blessing in disguise. I practically had a new home. Admittedly, I didn't get to see the hills of Connemara, but I had scaled Mount Everest in terms of humility.

Charlie and I sat on my new bed settee, drinking coffee and smoking tobacco, surveying my new surroundings. My daughter sat on the floor with a new toy I had bought her. It was a plastic tray with triangle-, square- and circle-shaped holes in it. It had accompanying plastic shapes to slot into the correct places. She spent a long time trying this shape and that, and got most of them in. We watched her as she diligently studied each one. Then she tried to force the triangle shape into the square hole and gave up.

She turned to me, still holding the triangle shape.

'That's just the way it is,' she sighed, her arms outstretched in a gesture of surrender. Then she quickly moved on to the next shape, not wasting a second more on something that didn't work.

Mmmm.

Wasn't it Dr Seuss who said: 'adults are obsolete children'?

5

I fell in love in a graveyard. Please don't ask me why. Only God knows the answer to such inexplicable mysteries. People fall in love in all kinds of strange places. It might have happened in a supermarket, a school house, or a pub. It just so happened that I found love in a burial ground. I hadn't been looking for love. In fact, had Michael been the last remaining male on earth, and thrown me the glad eye, I would have absconded.

Let's dispense with the preliminaries. This man was not my type. He was the antithesis of what I am normally attracted to in a man. I think that's why I initially felt it safe to be pals with him. In a trillion light-years, I could never have foreseen the possibility of romantic feelings developing between us. But I felt a comfortable easiness when in his company, and it lulled me into a false sense of security. Rock solid in my conviction that companionship was all we would ever share, I fell, even toppled, into the proverbial 'platonic friend' trap.

I had known Michael in the past. In fact, we had been neighbours and had grown up together as kids. Not exactly the guy next door, but near enough. He had spent seventeen years in New Zealand, and had returned to Ireland. Tragically, his best friend had died recently. I knew his best friend too, and had turned up at the funeral to offer my support. Michael was touched by this. He began to phone me; the odd time at first, then more frequently. Soon I began to meet him regularly, going for walks, cups of coffee.

I was standing next to Phil Lynott's plot in Sutton cemetery, sifting through the letters, poems and various other keepsakes that people had left on his grave. There was a strong wind in that open stretch, and strands of my long hair kept finding their way into my mouth. I glanced over and spotted Michael about two hundred feet away, on his hunkers, removing some weeds from around his friend's headstone.

He stood up and adjusted his jeans. Michael had lost a considerable amount of weight, so they were loose-fitting. He was yanking them up, tucking in his shirt and tightening his belt. I don't know what it was about the moment, or that spectacularly ordinary gesture, but that image of Michael has been permanently stapled to my brain cells. I knew in that instant that I loved him; it was as if some beautiful spirit of the angelic realm had walked right through me. It dawned on me: I was besotted with Michael.

There had been not one kiss, not one hug. Not even an accidental brushing of the shoulders had been exchanged. Michael had never passed a nodding remark about the scaly red patch on my left elbow, never mind made any sexual advances, and it was probably this that made him . . . appealing.

I hadn't seen it coming. All I knew was that when I was in his company, I felt quietly protected. There was an undeclared understanding between us. I came to expect his calls, which were daily and numerous. Michael pretty much dominated my phone. We often rambled through St Anne's Park, sauntered along Howth Harbour or strolled the seafront in Clontarf.

Michael was an old-style gentleman, courteous and respectful – qualities I found intriguing. He was paternal and protective without being patronising and also a terrific listener and had a sharp wit. Michael was a very capable man and was able to turn his hand to practically anything. He was a gifted salesman, a keen gardener and a superb cook; like me, he devoured books. Michael also had a cool-headedness and practicality that I lacked. I was attracted to that, because I had been dealt a poor hand in the chilly, calm and unemotional department. Two words, to be exact: drama, and queen.

Alcoholics don't think, they 'emote'. And I was blessed with an extremely passionate temperament because I was both artist and alcoholic – a truly rotten combination.

My emotions ran deeper than the elaborate underground of London's Tube stations, and I was intense. Michael, on the other hand, lacked any of my mercuriality. He was objective. So, for me, he possessed a refreshing rationale and reasoning that I admired.

Michael was tender and sensitive, and had a delicious warmth that made me feel as if I was being incubated in an impenetrable cotton-wool cocoon. One has to remember that my previous relationships had been turbulent. I had only ever attracted brutal, aggressive, controlling types, and had never experienced being treated as an equal. Dignified and respectful liaisons had evaded me, and of true intimacy I knew little. I was like the legendary lamb to the slaughter.

Michael was *always* quietly just there. I realise now that he had already marked his territory. I had, in fact, been his from the very moment he had set eyes on me.

As much as I would like to describe him, anonymity is the foundation upon which Alcoholics Anonymous was built, so I am prevented from doing this. So I will use a different kind of correlation. They say beauty is in the eye of the beholder. I will confirm that aphorism. In my eyes, he had the most beautiful face in the whole world. It became a bit of an ongoing banter between us, because I would make this statement matter-of-factly, several times a day. We might have been in the thick of a debate on politics, or a heavy discussion about the failing ozone layer, and I would jest: 'You still have the most beautiful face in the whole world.' This never failed to soften him, and bring that look of love into his eyes.

He listened to me intently, as Charlie did, and that was something I had longed for in a relationship. He was everything I could wish for, and it all seemed too good to be true. How right I was. Michael had one flaw and one flaw only: he was an alcoholic and heroin addict, and was struggling to stay clean.

Now any other normal person (or '*normies*', as Charlie referred to them) would have broken their tibia in the quest to escape, but I didn't. I was in love with Michael, long before our relationship turned into a full-blown romance. The spell was cast, and my fate was set in stone. In retrospect, I realise that Michael had not chosen to fall in love with me either, but we were both human. I was smitten, and suffering from what I now identify as 'happiness disorder'.

We had been meeting each other for weeks, and Michael had always been polite. While it was all innocent and respectful, there came a stage where I craved much more. I had entertained the ghastly idea that I had interpreted the whole thing wrongly. The poor man didn't feel anything for me, other than a kinship. Michael *was* a chivalrous man, but I guess he too had reached the 'Excuse me, but I desperately wish to rip every fragment of clothing from your body' juncture, because sure enough the night came when he finally made his true intentions clear in one swift and beautiful gesture.

We had been out for coffee, chatting and laughing, with a number of friends. Outside the coffee shop, we all made to say our goodbyes. One male friend gave me a bear hug and a rather cheeky kiss on the forehead. I don't know what got into him, but something sure as hell got into Michael. He stepped up to me, lifted my head and held my face in both his hands. He smiled, a knowing smile, staring right into my Bambi-like eyes, and then he kissed me. And again, this time hard and furious. The chemistry was intense. The kiss had long ended, but my eyes were shut fast. I was swaying like a palm tree in a hurricane, my lips pursed and guppy-like, full of expectation. I was dumbfounded, but suddenly I understood. This was Michael's way of making a statement. It was not only for my benefit, but to enlighten all and sundry about our connection. I was, from that day on, completely his, heart and soul.

Michael had been struggling with recovery for the best part

of ten years, achieving periodic bouts of abstinence. Six weeks, two months, and then a slip. Then six weeks, then three months, before another slip. One binge would be on alcohol, and then he would stop drinking, only to take up heroin. As soon as he managed to give up heroin, he would go back drinking. This seesawing vicious circle went on and on. I never believed for one second that he wouldn't eventually recover fully. I knew he was doing his best. He never stopped going to meetings, never stopped trying.

I spoke to him at length about how I had achieved sobriety, and shared with him what Charlie had shared with me. I did my best to help, minding him while he went through the drying-out process, and sat with him while he detoxified again and again. I witnessed him in the DTs and observed him in heroin withdrawal. This was all excruciatingly painful to watch, but I simply could not give up on him – despite being told by well-meaning friends that I should.

When he was clean and sober, Michael made supernatural recoveries in very short periods of time. He would miraculously pull himself up, get a job and a sponsor, and start looking healthy and fit. Bizarrely, it always seemed just at that point when he was making an immense improvement that he would slip off the wagon again. I was frustrated as to why this kept happening. It was the voice of addiction infusing him with its dirty lies, telling him that he was OK and that he could handle a few drinks, that he would get away with it. Of course, he never did. The chain reaction of taking the poison reignited the compulsion, and the addict dance would begin again. Each slip was more harrowing than the preceding one, but I was not deterred. I was not giving up on him.

Michael was pushing forty years of age now, and I was thirty-five. Time was running out. I showed him how I prayed. Many's a time I knelt down beside him and prayed with him. I became quite close to his mother – a wonderful, spiritual, loving woman whom he adored, and vice versa. Often we supported each other when Michael went on a bender and disappeared for days. They were torturous times for all concerned, and nothing anyone did seemed to help.

I was still attending to the kids and my job, but the strain was beginning to show. My babysitter was a wonderfully kind and accommodating woman, so I mostly chose to meet Michael in his place. At the time, he lived in a tiny bedsit in Portmarnock. Thankfully the children never witnessed Michael when he was drinking or on drugs. I was extremely protective of them, and refused to allow Michael near the house when he was in a withdrawal period.

At other times, I would get an emergency call and go looking for him, finding him passed out down a laneway, or in a DART station. There were many calls for the ambulance, the doctor, trips to the accident and emergency department, overdoses, drying-out sessions, rehabilitation, treatment centres, halfway houses – on and on it went.

It always ended the same way. Michael would stop periodically, only to slide further into the gutter the next time. One night I was on my way to a meeting in a friend's car. Michael staggered out onto the road, drunk, veering and unaware of where he was. Cars beeped and swerved to avoid him. I was so upset, I couldn't go to the meeting, and the inevitable hospital run followed. The doctors were getting used to Michael's regular appearances, and I could see the impatience in their eyes and the exasperation in their voices. He was obstreperous and abusive, while they tried in vain to help him. He had become a public nuisance, a menace, wasting their precious time. I could understand their disgust.

I stood by, powerless, while he mumbled incoherently, then suddenly burst into tears. He paced the floors night after night, begging for the compulsion to leave him. Only now, Michael had added other chemicals to the deadly concoction. He was abusing benzodiazepines, copious amounts of codeine, and boxes of painkillers. He needed Valium and Librium to come down, and a cocktail of other medications to get up. He knew every drug there was – his knowledge was so vast that he could have had a degree in pharmacology.

I would respond to his drunken calls and rush to his assistance. I often found him crawling about on his hands and knees, hallucinating, talking to himself, searching desperately for just one more drink. I would call a doctor, or his mother or brother, and get medication. Often I bought food, or left money for the rent. On occasion I had to buy him alcohol, so he wouldn't take an alcoholic fit. I had to in order to keep him alive.

I heard his terrified shrieks, as illusory goblins and demons stalked his every move. I watched him tear at his skin till it bled, while 'leeches' and 'insects' feasted on his flesh. I looked on while he vomited blood and bile, and diarrhoea ran down his leg. I watched him go through high fevers, desperate delusions and horrifying delirium. The alcohol and heroin seeped from his pores, drenching the sheets on the bed, and leaving in its wake a vile stench.

I was constantly tired, feeling drained and depressed. My children were spending more time with my babysitter than me, so they weren't seeing much of a mother either. Michael seemed to be getting worse. At one stage he was thrown out of his bedsit and began to sleep in an abandoned, burnt-out car. There I was, nurse, psychiatrist, counsellor and sponsor. Instead of helping him, my interference was only enabling him to continue in his addiction. At one stage it was suggested to me that I was, in fact, helping to kill him. I failed to see how this could be. It just didn't make sense. It was impossible for me to let go. I would have done anything to keep him alive, spending hours on my knees in churches, lighting candles and saying novenas.

Charlie knew I was in trouble, but was reluctant to offer his opinion. As a sponsor, it was not his job to have an opinion on my private relationships. I dodged his phone calls, and avoided meetings where I knew he'd be. I realise how much this must have hurt him. Not only the rejection, but watching me fall further into a relationship that was becoming impossible to manage. It must have been very painful for him to watch my downfall and be powerless to stop it. Despite my best efforts to avoid him, I found myself coerced into facing him whether I wanted to or not.

I was visiting the local library one afternoon. Apart from churches, it was the only place where I could find solace. I was poring over a book about addiction. I had several more under my arm, to take out.

I became aware of someone standing next to me.

'Any good?' the gravelly voice asked.

'Are you stalking me now?' I asked, without even having to turn around.

'I had no idea you were here.'

I turned, and knew by the look on his face that Charlie was telling the truth.

It was a coincidence – or 'Godincidence', as I like to refer to them now.

'I could write a better book myself. I am appalled at the amount of books I have read about addiction, and just how inaccurate they are – and insincere too.'

'Maybe you should write a book about addiction yourself.'

'Fat chance.'

He picked up a book entitled *When You Lose Someone You Love*.

'Someone die?' I asked.

'The Brown Rat. He passed on.'

'Aw.'

'I know. I'm bereft.'

'What are the funeral arrangements?'

'Cremation. In Finglas dump, tomorrow.'

'I'll send a wreath.'

He smiled a half-smile.

'What's been happening?' he asked nonchalantly. 'I haven't seen you at meetings.'

'I'm at my other meetings.'

'Humph. You got time for a coffee?'

I really didn't want to go for a coffee. I didn't want him to know anything about Michael, or that my nervous system was shot to hell, but I went.

We ambled out of the library, and headed to the coffee shop in Donaghmede. I was obsessed with thoughts of Michael. Is he dead in a ditch? Has he overdosed? Has someone beaten him up and mugged him? Has he food? Is he in a hospital? Is he in bed with some other woman?

Charlie bought two coffees, and we found a free table. A waitress came along minutes later and placed two fat cream cakes in front of us.

'Jesus, no wonder the waitresses here are all fat,' Charlie said.

'Charlie, that's prejudice.'

'I'm just saying, you must need to be fifteen stone minimum to get an interview in this gaff.'

'That's so rude.'

'Add another two stone to actually become an employee. Want some cake?'

'Please keep your voice down. Where are your manners?'

'Want some *fucking* cake?' he rephrased.

I sighed heavily while staring at the cream cake. Charlie had already digested one. Before I could take a stab at mine, it too was in his mouth.

I stared absently into my coffee cup, as if somehow it might yield the details of my sordid future. Charlie lit a smoke and started to swirl his coffee. My thoughts swirled too. The silence between us was unbearable. All picture, no sound. I wanted to talk, but didn't know how to start. All sense of personal identity had been lost in the bid to save Michael's life. There hadn't been time to notice how sick I had become.

'I was in love once,' Charlie said, nodding. 'Well, I *thought* I was in love. I was pissed drunk at the time. She was gorgeous, until the lights came on.' He took out a well-used handkerchief and wiped the gunge off his face. 'When the pub is closing, the lights come on, and you realise you're snogging an extra-terrestrial. She looked like a horse. I didn't know whether to offer her a cup of tea or a nosebag.'

'Was she in love with you?'

'No, I don't think so.'

'What makes you so sure?'

'Believe me, I'm sure. Last time I saw her, she hurled a cauliflower at me, then dragged me to the door, and said: "Get the fuck out, you fat evil pig."'

'But you're only nine stone.'

'I know. She was so angry, she just couldn't think of anything else to say.'

'What did you do that made her fly into such a rage?'

'It was more about what I *failed* to do. I hadn't a clue

about love then. I always equated love with sexual attraction,' he said, cupping his face in his hands.

'Are you trying to tell me something here? Like you're attracted to horses and stuff?'

'I'm trying to tell you that I had such low self-worth, I didn't think I deserved any better.'

I winced.

'There's all kinds of love, isn't there? There's the love for a child, for a parent, a friend, a lover, a spouse . . . .' He let the last word linger. I was surprised by this little show of vulnerability. I knew that Charlie had been widowed for a considerable number of years. He hardly ever referred to personal family issues. He also rarely spoke about his children or grandchildren, because he was fiercely protective of them. I respected that.

'Then there's falling in love. Now that's the real bastard. Someone once said, love is an understanding between two fools. It's a bit like emotional vertigo. You're dizzy with elation one minute, and then plunged into despair the next.'

'Did you ever really fall in love?'

'Oh yes, every ten seconds. All I had to do was brush shoulders with a woman and I was in love. I once even fell in love with a schizophrenic ballet dancer. More of a Nutcracker Suite than a Swan Lake, if you get my meaning.'

'You're making a mockery of me.'

'I'm talking about me, not you. Not everything is about you.'

I shut up.

'Anyway, once bitten, twice as likely to spiral into chemical depression, as I always say. I used to think my heart was for pumping blood around. The longest journey I had to make was from this, to this.' He pointed to his head and then to his heart.

'We can lick thumbs on that.'

Charlie broke into a bad fit of coughing.

'Have you been to a doctor about that?'

'With my eighty-a-day habit? Don't be lame.' He barked heavily into a cloth handkerchief.

'Well, you should: you might need antibiotics. It sounds like you have a bad chest infection.'

'I've been coughing since I came out of my mother's womb.'

He gave me a disdainful look, and then lit up again.

'So who is he?' he asked, head down.

'Who is who?'

'The poor unfortunate bastard you're in love with.'

'An old friend.'

'Is he good to you?'

'Yes.'

'Do you like him?'

'I love him.'

'I know, but do you *like* him? That's more important.'

I didn't understand.

'Yes, I do like him.'

'So why are you so miserable-looking?'

'I'm not miserable. I'm very happy actually.'

'Are ya? You've a face on ya that could haunt a house.'

'It's difficult.'

'Humph.'

'He keeps slipping.'

'Slipping?'

'I don't know what I'm doing wrong.'

'Wait. Is this guy an alcoholic?'

'I *have* tried to help him, but nothing works.'

'Jesus. An active one?'

'I love him so much, and he's killing himself.'

'And do you want him to take you with him?'

'Huh?'

'Because that's what's happening!'

Charlie took an empty glass off the table and held it up. He poured his cup of coffee into it.

'Let's just say that this glass represents your recovery.'

He picked up another glass that was empty.

'And this is his.'

He slowly began to pour the coffee into the empty glass.

'Your energy is going into his recovery, and he's draining you.'

By the time he had finished pouring, my glass was empty.

'See what's happening?'

'I'm OK. If you're suggesting I'm going to take a drink, you're wrong.'

'There isn't enough coffee to fill the two glasses.' He banged them together to emphasise the point. 'Are you vision-impaired as well as dense?'

'I can see perfectly well, thank you.'

'Something has got to give, and it's you who is doing the giving.'

'But he loves me.'

'How can he really love you in active addiction? For Christ's sake, he doesn't even know who he is.'

'He knows who he is – that's the bloody problem!'

'No, he doesn't. He hasn't a clue who he is. Think of him like you would a married man.'

'He's not married.'

'Oh, but he is. To his addiction. His first love is drugs and alcohol. Put simply, his addiction can be seen as the other woman.'

'He's always been faithful to me.'

'Mmmm.'

'He's never been abusive, never lifted a hand to me – not like the other bastards.'

'Uh huh.'

'He's kind, affectionate and warm. All my other relationships were so bad in comparison.'

'I don't want to know about your relationships from the day of the Flood. Tell that to your therapist.'

'He is thoughtful and considerate,' I insisted, getting more and more agitated.

'Yes. It's very thoughtful and considerate to have you awake all night worrying, while he's in total oblivion.'

'But . . . .'

'And his affection and warmth are evident when you're trying to juggle a job and two kids and AA meetings, and you're waiting for him to come and cut the grass – only he won't make it, because he's passed out stone cold in a laneway somewhere.'

'He can't help it. He's sick.'

'We're all fucking sick.'

'He treats me with dignity.'

'Yes. He fucks you. Then fucks off.'

'Hey!'

'Such devout dignity.'

'And he treats me with the utmost respect.'

'Wham, bam, thank you, ma'am. Yes, I know. The personification of respect!'

'It's not like that.'

'Not like what? Am I missing something here?'

'He doesn't mean to hurt me.'

'Ah. There you go.'

'What?'

'He *is* hurting you.'

'I never said that.'

'Well, it doesn't exactly take a psychiatrist to figure it out.'

'So now you're Sigmund Freud? I suppose you're an expert on love, too?'

'I don't know much about love, that's true, but I sure as hell know what it isn't.'

'Well, elaborate then, oh enlightened one.'

'Obsession? Great sex? Infatuation? All red herrings.'

Fuck. The sex *was* great. It was dripping with desperation, and verging on the violent. The type of lovemaking you engage in when you're making up after a row – lots of breath-defying expressions of exclusive and inextinguishable love.

I was fixated. As we were speaking, I clung tight to my mobile phone. I couldn't live without it, and got withdrawal symptoms if I didn't look at it every five seconds. My forefinger and thumb had repetitive strain injury from texting. I wasn't telling Charlie any of that, though.

'Your great love for this man hasn't made a damn bit of difference when it comes to his addiction. He chooses drugs and alcohol over you, over everything. You're powerless. You can't save him. How can he get well when you keep bailing him out? You're standing in his way; you're delaying his recovery and jeopardising your own. You think that if you love him enough, if you try harder, if you love him just a little bit more, he'll stop, right?'

I nodded.

'Did the love of your children or your family stop you?'

'No.'

'Then what makes you think it will stop him?'

'I don't know.'

'Does caring for this man make you feel good, worthy, needed?'

'Yes.' I hated admitting it, but it did.

'That's not love,' he said emphatically.

'Then what fucking is? I have never loved a man the way I love him.'

The waitress arrived with more coffee.

'I love everything about him,' I said. 'I love the very bones of him. I've never felt like this about any man. You can't tell me I don't love him. I know I do.'

'If you love him that much, then surely his happiness means a lot to you. You must want him to get well. You do, don't you? Don't you want him to be free and happy?'

'I would do anything for him, anything at all. I told you, I love him.'

'Do you love him enough to leave him?'

The silence hung between us, like some African killer bee.

'You are the one who is supposed to be in recovery, right? You have to be the bigger character here. Leave him. Show him how much you really love him. Let him go. Detach with love. If you don't, you don't love him.'

'I can't leave him; it would be too hard.'

'Usually, whatever is the hardest thing for you to do tends to be the right thing to do.'

I wasn't interested in the rights and wrongs of my actions. Hearing the truth was something I was out to avoid at all costs.

'And I suppose he doesn't love me either? He tells me he loves me every day.'

'Humph.'

He tipped his hat and leaned his arms on the table, staring right into my face.

'You know the best way to judge anyone's true character? Watch what they do, not what they say. What he says and how he behaves doesn't exactly match up, does it? If he is unreliable, letting you down at a moment's notice, leaving you for days on end crying and worrying. Can you really call that loving, caring behaviour? I think if you truly apply that rule, you will soon see that this great love of yours is an ego-feeding fest for you, and a delusional distraction on his part. It will end in extreme heartache, at the very least. Worst-case scenario? You'll kill each other. If you want to throw away all you have worked so hard for, you couldn't take a shorter, swifter route.'

I wasn't able for that. I jumped up and grabbed my bag.

'You know what's wrong with you?' I said. 'You're jealous!'

Charlie adjusted his hat and coughed into his handkerchief.

'Watch what they do, not what they say,' he repeated, unfazed by my outburst. 'When you have dug yourself a hole this big, the best thing to do is throw away the spade.'

'And I thought you were a friend.'

'The truth always hurts. I will never tell you what you want to hear, only what you *need* to hear. That's the deal.'

Charlie stood up and put on his coat. I wasn't listening. I walked away before he had the chance to do it to me first.

6

I am not sure, to this day, who left whom. I would like to think I left Michael, but the truth is that he left me. In fact, every time he drank and took drugs, he left me. On several occasions I had tried to end it, and then I would inadvertently pick up the phone again. It was an addiction in itself. The relationship had made me very sick. The sad truth is that I had begun to resent, indeed detest, Michael.

My behaviour had become abusive and controlling. The rows were more frequent, more volatile, and my temper flared at the slightest sign of mistrust. I demanded to know every second of the day where he was, what he was doing and who he was with. In short, I pestered him, watching his every move. Michael, in turn, was repelled by my habitual intrusion and became more tight-lipped and distant. The gap between us became wider and wider.

I had come to hate his addiction, not him, but I could no longer distinguish one from the other. The lines had become muddled, and I failed to separate the two realities. What I really despised was his illness, not Michael. Both had fused, turning into one big blur.

I had suffered from bouts of depression in the past, but now my secondary illness returned with a vengeance. Despair became my daily companion. I still clung to the delusion that it would all somehow magically right itself; if I waited long enough, I might come up with a new past. But grief is a process. It's lengthy and frustrating because of the 'two steps forward, four steps back' routine. It's only now that I comprehend the expressions 'mad with grief' and 'madly in love'. Grief is a kind of long-suffering insanity. It would be so much easier if you could take a tablet or capsule, like you de-worm a cat – one dose cures all. The only cure is time. No one can say how long or how short their particular brand of derail-ment will be. Grief is a law unto itself, and I was no exception to it.

Breaking up with Michael provided me with the Rolls-Royce of excuses to go off the deep end. I took his addiction personally, interpreting it as rejection, and I couldn't find any measure of acceptance about it. Having once been extremely close to his mother, I now found that she too was dissociating, removing herself further and further from me. That hurt just as much. It felt as if I had suddenly become the horned beast, and Michael had sprouted wings and a halo.

The truth is, of course, that Michael was an addict before he met me, while he was with me, and after we broke up. I could not weather this seemingly convenient flipping of the coin. Suddenly, *I* had become the problem. The loss of Michael was overwhelming in itself, but now I felt I had been judged unfairly. It seemed as if what I had tried to do to help him was instantly forgotten. While Michael's behaviour was excused and labelled as sick, no one seemed to notice that I was also sick. A lot of it had to do with perpetually having to deal with his addiction. I was practically a hospital job myself. The double-whammy curse that had played havoc with my life was back to mock me again. I was grief-stricken and suicidal. Having lost Michael, I lost myself. I wasn't able to cope with the twin fatalities.

The rejection was unbearable. I felt as though I was being isolated and punished at the same time. I already had my own issues, and these reared their ugly heads like the Medusa reincarnate. So my response to the social leprosy, which I thought had been forced on me, was to exhibit even more extreme reactions. At times my behaviour was nothing short of bizarre. I was distraught, and had no idea how to express the distress in a healthy manner. I did and said things I will regret forever.

It was suggested to me more than once to start attending Al-Anon meetings as well as AA meetings. Al-Anon meetings are specifically designed to help friends, relatives and families of someone who is an addict or alcoholic, but I wasn't sure they would welcome the enemy (an alcoholic) into their midst. I was so low, and really didn't know where to turn. I cried constantly, and could have filled a swimming pool with my tears. Michael and I still bumped into each other at AA meetings – which made the pain even more intense. The opportunity for substantial healing was scant. As soon as I saw his face, the wound would be ripped of its stitching, leaving me to bleed again.

Charlie and I were sitting in the old café on the seafront.

'Someone said to go to an Al-Anon meeting,' I said nonchalantly. 'What do you think?'

'Al-Anon, Nar-Anon. Do you know, in the States they have Emotions-Anon?' he mused.

'I don't want to go. It's the parliamentary wing of AA. Enemy territory.'

'Then they have Overeaters-Anon, Cocaine-Anon, Gamblers-Anon.'

'His mother will be there. I couldn't hack that.'

'Women-who-love-too-much-Anon. Men-who-hate-women-Anon. Women-who-follow-men-to-Men-who-hate-women-Anon. It gets very fucking confusing.'

'How could I possibly talk honestly in front of her? She doesn't know half the stuff he's put me through.'

'Next thing there will be a Dumped-by-AA-member-Anon! Or wait, maybe they have that already . . . .'

I started to bawl into my coffee.

He handed me a snotty handkerchief and I blew into it.

'You'll meet someone else,' he offered gently.

'I don't want anyone else. Don't you understand that? He's the one I want.'

'What you want and what you need are two completely different things, Cathy. He's no good for you, and you're no good for him either.'

'Now you're playing God.'

'Humph.'

'I can't cope with this emotional pain. I would rather have my legs sawn off.'

It was a genuine revelation.

'The good news is: it will pass. The bad news is: it takes time.'

'But how *much* time? I think I'll never be myself again.'

'It will last as long as you keep clinging to those handlebars.'

When you've truly learned the lesson of letting go, it will let go of you.'

'How many more lessons?'

Charlie broke into a hail of coughing, excused himself, and went outside. I could see him through the window, hawking into his handkerchief.

'Sorry about that,' he said when he returned. 'Damn cough has me tormented.'

'It has me tormented too. Will you please go and see a doctor?'

'No. I would rather have my teeth pulled by a gynaecologist.'

'But you're not well.'

'It's just some bug – a viral thingamajig. It will run its course in its own time.'

He looked pale and tired, but I knew it was useless to persist. When Charlie had his mind made up, there was no changing it.

Days turned into weeks, weeks into months. I was still grieving. If anything, the pain seemed to intensify. Its presence was unremitting. I fell into a deep depression.

I went back to my own doctor, who prescribed anti-depressants. This was nothing to be particularly alarmed about. Having been diagnosed with depression on and off since I was seventeen, there were times when I had to resort to medication to kick-start my dormant endorphins. Enlisting the assistance of a very good counsellor also helped a bit. I went once a week and poured my heart out. However, neither the anti-depressants nor the counselling did much to alleviate the gnawing sense of loss. I ached for Michael morning, noon and night.

People were sick of listening to my tale of woe. Understandably, friends felt that my period of mourning had well passed its sell-by date and I should have recovered sufficiently. Well-meaning pals passed off the predictable combination of pacifying pleasantries. Statements like 'There's more fish in the sea' and 'This time next year you won't even remember his face' did little to lessen my distress. Michael's face still loomed before me; as hard as I tried to eradicate the past, my heart conspired against me. I simply could not forget.

Meanwhile, in my world, circumstances had improved somewhat. I was now working full-time in a local Credit Union, and I really enjoyed the job. The working hours were long, but I was grateful for the adult company. It kept me occupied and helped me meet the Santa Claus list of financial demands of two dependants. It left little time for me to dwell on the plight of my bruised and crestfallen heart.

Acting on friends' advice, I tried dating other men. Initially, the relationships started out well, but they always seemed to end in remarkably similar circumstances. I would succumb to the 'comparison' game, and Michael won out every time. That parking slot in my heart still read 'reserved'. I was carrying a torch, as they say. In fact, the torch was large enough to initiate the opening ceremony at the Olympics. All the men I dated seemed to know instinctively that I was 'not available' emotionally.

In hindsight, I hurt many men. Sadly, there were one or two who did actually fall in love with me. Good, honest, decent people, but they always had to contend with the ghost of another man. This was appallingly unjust. One particular man comes to mind. A prolific writer/moviemaker whom I happened to meet on my travels. He seemed to be made for me. Family and friends had us betrothed after five dates. We made a very compatible pair, and he treated me like a queen. The relationship was all I could have asked for, but it was polka-dotted with petty disputes and spates of sullen silences – all of which indicated that a part of me was still bound by the preceding affair. He was a wonderfully witty, romantic man, and to say he doted on me was an understatement. He lived in Spain – a place I had come to call my second home. We commuted between Dublin and Spain every month.

Periodically, I would get a call from Michael, and a brief reunion ensued. It never lasted, because it couldn't. Each step backwards only encouraged further confusion. It was very unfair on my new boyfriend, but he was blessed with an abundance of tolerance, and hoped that these fleeting retreats back into Michael-land would eventually fizzle out. The plan was that we would settle down into a more committed relationship and that I would eventually move to Spain with my children to be closer to him.

After one week-long visit to his beautiful home, the whole thing disintegrated. He simply could not take any more. He sat me down and laid out his cards on the table. 'Cathy, I can't share you with someone else. Especially some ghost I can't even see.' Those words marked the end of yet another potentially good relationship. I was so frustrated because I didn't want to feel anything for Michael myself.

It was 1996, and I had been sober for four years. Finally, I came face to face with my second rock bottom. One grey and dank December evening, I descended into what I now call 'the suicidal psalm'. I hadn't stopped going to meetings, but my head had. I heard nothing any more, and was filled with a crippling indifference. My brain had been kicking the shit out of me for so long, I felt that I simply could not continue. I went through my mobile-phone numbers, wondering whom to contact, and knowing that everyone had grown tired of my incessant tale of adversity.

Isn't it amazing what a fractured heart can ruin for life – a song, a smell, or a particular place? I still crumbled at the opening notes of Dido's 'White Flag'. St Anne's Park and the seafront were forbidden walking zones. The scent of Youth Dew perfume or freshly mown grass plunged me into sorrow – right back into the pain-pen. I wanted to reach out, but couldn't. I felt imprisoned – sentenced to a life of yearning for something that would always elude me. The chances of enjoying another relationship seemed non-existent. I felt destined to be alone for ever. Pieces of me were eroding. The loneliness cloaked me like a second skin. I never did relish being unaccompanied in my pain, and always found someone else to take along for the ride.

Reluctantly, I dialled Charlie's number.

'Hey.'

'How are you?'

'Shite.'

'Yeah?' Munch, munch.

'I want to die,' I wailed.

Munch, munch, slobber, slobber.

'I'm going to kill myself.'

'Mmmm.'

'Are you there?'

'Yes.' Chomp, chomp. 'Actually, I'm having my dinner right now. Tell you what, I'll call you back in an hour.'

'What?'

Munch, slobber, munch.

'Don't bother your fucking arse!' I screamed, slamming down the phone.

Obviously Brussel sprouts were more important than my imminent death. I even bet that while I was taking my last breath he would be loading up the dishwasher. No one cared if I lived or died. I called my babysitter and asked her to come and mind the children while I went out. I had my coat on when she arrived.

'Going to a meeting?' she asked.

'Erm. Yes. There's one in Howth. I may go there,' I mumbled, trying hard to obscure my tumescent eyelids.

'Are you OK?'

'Sure, I'm fine,' I lied.

I fumbled out the front door in great haste. I had no intention of going to any meeting, and had no idea where I was going, or what I was doing. Such is the doctrine of the 'suicidal psalm'. Its distorted prompts drew me deeper and deeper into its lethal clutches. Emotional anaesthesia seized me. In hindsight, it stands to reason that I had no other option but to disconnect. The pain had reached overdose status; its toxicity was choking me. Subconsciously, I had walked out of my own autobiography.

I found myself at Howth Junction DART station, not really aware of which side of the platform I wanted to be on. No longer dictating my own fate, I stood for an eternity, just gazing at the interconnecting tracks. Eventually, buying a one-way ticket to Howth Station, I stepped onto the DART in a trance. The DART was overcrowded. Christmas shoppers returning from the city centre were crammed in like canned tuna. Some children were sitting on the floor. I had to stand against the door, clutching the overhead rail.

It seemed that every family had their proportionate quota of members, i.e. a mother, a father and x number of kids. I didn't have that. I didn't have a partner. The man I loved did not want me, and I did not want anyone else. What was the point of being sober? What was the point in any of this wretched existence? I was branded like the sheep on the Wicklow mountains. I had a catalogue of socially unacceptable labels that would always make me an oddball: alcoholic, single parent, depressive – no one would want me. If this was sobriety, if this was life, it harboured no significance for me any more.

I wandered aimlessly through Howth village, up the Balscadden Road, and along the cliffs. (I used to go there a lot when I was a teenager. On Sundays, my school friends and I climbed up all the way and made the long scenic trek to the other side.) It was perilously dark, and the meandering, tumble-down footpath was only inches from the precipice. I looked over the side into a black abyss, where the frothy crowns of raging breakers sprayed against the rocks. The angry squawk of flocking seagulls penetrated the desolate surroundings. Even the natural elements were keening. Like a ghostly orchestra, they performed in tandem with my own brokenness.

I carefully made my way back down the cliffs, passing Yeats's little cottage, and went towards the iridescent lights of the village. I didn't want to go home. I headed towards the pier. There was nobody about, and the soft, hypnotic solitude lured me along. The pier was polish-black, illuminated only by the star-spangled blanket above. The moon hung in the heavens like a basin of liquid gold. The wind was blade-sharp, and I wrapped my scarf about my face, trying to protect myself from its cutting bite. Suicidal thoughts continued to invade me. Their irrational overtones had me over a barrel. I thought about my anti-depressants. I had a month's supply of them in my bag. What if I took them all? Would it be enough to finish me off? What if I hadn't enough and woke up in some hospital? No, that wouldn't do.

I kept walking.

I reached the end of the pier and lit a cigarette. The caustic wind whipped around me. The open sea pulverised the moored yachts, its current brutal, yet hypnotically inviting. The end of the pier was sectioned off. I ran my hands along the heavy, rusty chains that coiled like snakes from one cement pillar to the next. All I had to do was step over them to be free.

I took out my mobile phone and dialled Michael's number.

His answering machine came on. His phone was switched off. I knew what that meant. He was off drugging and drinking. I think I left a message, but I'm pretty sure he never heard it. The signal was weak at the end of the pier, and the wind would have drowned out anything I said anyway. Besides, I knew that Michael didn't give a damn if I was alive or dead – and frankly, neither did I.

I moved closer to the edge. The punishing gusts of wind made me sway. It all seemed so easy. To just put my foot out and walk. I would be instantly swept away by the raging tide. That, coupled with the intense cold, would have me dead within minutes. My children's faces swam before me.

Christmases. Putting a big boot-mark on the landing and sprinkling talcum powder around it, making a trail of the footprints into the kids' bedrooms. Their squeals of delight in the early hours of Christmas Day. 'Mam, quick! Look, Mam, look! Santa was here!'

Birthday parties. Making an ice cream Teenage Mutant Ninja Turtle cake. It took five hours, but was worth every second, just to see my son's face light up.

Dental appointments. Holding my daughter's hand while she had an extraction. Squeezing all the love I could muster into her. The chipped pink Barbie nailpaint on her chubby little fingers. The vice-like grip of them. Smiling into her petrified face.

Keeping her eyes locked on to mine, so she knew I was right there beside her and not going to move one inch.

Operations. Heading down to the operating theatre in the Mater Private for my son's four-hour ear surgery. He was only five years old at the time. Him on the gurney in a gown, vulnerable and trying to be a man. The flicker of his smiling, bright blue eyes as the anaesthesia started to take effect. 'I love you, Mam. I'll . . . be . . . back . . . .' – said in his best Arnie Schwarzenegger voice.

Schooling. My daughter's school report. Skipping the grades section and hurrying to the remarks about her behaviour. 'Model student. Friendly. Mannerly. Always defends the underdog!' Oh, the pride! My son, having the courage to rent the book *The Hobbit* from the school library and putting up with six weeks of being tagged 'gay' and a 'snob'. How he didn't give in to the subtle bullying and even went back to borrow *Lord of the Rings*.

All the 'firsts'. My son learning to ride a two-wheeler bike. Weeks and weeks of going up and down the road, falling off – bruised elbows, grazed knees. Then the day he got it, and I just happened to be standing on the porch. He whizzed past with a clatter of children running alongside, egging him on, yahooing and yelping encouragement. The wind in his hair, his tracksuit bottoms ballooning out, his cheeks flushed with pride.

My daughter's first steps. How she had clung precariously to the front room armchair first, letting go with one hand. Then two. Then she wobbled her way over to the couch, the last few steps turning into a frantic run. How she grabbed hold of the couch cushion and fell flat on her bottom, bursting into a torrent of giggles.

I thought about their little faces. They zoomed in and out, at various ages: when they were born, when I first held them, their first teeth – which I had kept in a box – their identity bracelets, locks of their hair, the folders of art and drawings and scribbled poems, the crammed photograph albums. The vaccinations, the tonsillitis, the grommets, the whooping cough.

While the images assaulted me, the 'suicidal psalm' made sure to remove any semblance of my contribution towards their stability. It erased any of the positive influences I might have had on their lives. It didn't allow me to think about what kind of legacy I would leave behind if I took my own life. Instead, it argued opposing factors, prompting me to execute the contrary. Its defence counsel was well-rehearsed, well-researched and very persuasive.

Perhaps they would be better off with someone else? They would have their father to parent them, and their extended families to help. They would get stability, routine, emotional balance. They would inherit the house and be financially secure. Most of all, they wouldn't have to endure me and my illness any more.

I could not see that I had achieved anything in my so-called recovery. While I could remember all the above incidents of their childhoods, I genuinely could not feel my own contribution to their growth. Nor could I see my own kindness, generosity or caring soul. There was nothing good about me. My usefulness as a human being had shrivelled up, like when you throw a crisp bag onto an open fire.

I had forgotten that I had stopped drinking. That I was, in fact, a very conscientious and responsible mother and a staunchly loyal and reliable friend. Most of all, it had slipped my mind that I had managed to arrest my disease and sidestep the fatal diagnosis of alcoholism. I had forgotten Charlie's words: 'How you're doing and how you're feeling are two entirely different things.' The 'suicidal psalm' was wrapping up its rebuttal. I moved closer to the edge. I was only seconds away from oblivion. I made the sign of the cross and asked God to forgive me for what I was about to do.

I heard the clip-clop of boots on the pier. Hurried steps. Then a cough. The boots arrived beside me, tipping over the edge in alignment with my own.

'It's fucking dark down there,' Charlie said, as we both stood staring down into the black chasm. 'Bet it's ice cold as well. Freeze the arse off ya.'

'Why don't you just leave me alone?'

'I will, as soon as ya jump. I just want to make sure you actually do it.'

'Don't mock me.'

'I'm not mocking. Here, I'll give you me coat and shoes. That way you'll sink quicker.'

'Why don't you tie a rock around my foot while you're at it?'

We stood like two fools, staring down at the sea and wobbling in the wind.

'Did you ever hear the story about the guy who confessed all his past sins to a priest?'

'I don't want to hear your damn stories.'

'The priest told him he was forgiven, and that God had gathered up all his sins and put them into a huge big plastic bag, and thrown it into the sea.'

'I don't want to know any of this.'

'And then God went and made a big wooden plaque, a sign, and he hammered the sign into the sand beside where he had thrown the bag – and the sign said "No fishing".'

'Well, there sure aren't any fucking signs around here,' I said.

Charlie looked right and then left.

'What exactly did you expect? The Archangel Michael on a chariot?' he barked loudly into his fist, then thumped his chest hard.

I shrugged. 'How the hell did you find me?'

'I had a hunch. I came out here myself fifteen years ago to do the same thing you're contemplating now.'

'You're lying.'

'I am not! I did actually jump, but me foot caught in the life-belt rope and I got stuck, just under there,' he said, pointing.

'You're just trying to talk me out of it.'

'I was flapping about, gulping for air, like some giant salmon.'

'Stop it.'

'I was supposed to be killing meself, and I was screaming me lungs out for someone to help me. The fire brigade had to be called and all me clothes cut off me, before they could get me out. They reefed me out by me legs, the bollox frozen off me.'

I moved a little closer to the edge.

'When your body hits the water, the cold is shocking. It takes your breath away. Makes you think of those poor bastards who drowned in the *Titanic*. Took them fifteen minutes to die. That's a long time. Slow, agonizing, painful, just floating around in sub-zero temperatures, waiting for your lungs to freeze up.'

I stood there thinking about that.

'If I had been on the *Titanic*, I would have found the nearest gun and shot meself,' Charlie said eventually.

'Why?'

'Why? Because I'm such a fucking coward.'

A huge wave smashed against the wall, licking against the tips of our boots. I was automatically tempted to move backwards, but didn't. Charlie did. He stood silently behind me.

'I'm not afraid to die,' I said. 'It's living that terrifies me.'

I thought about myself on the *Titanic*, and what I would have done. I realised I wouldn't have been much more of a hero than Charlie, and that he had been honest and humble enough to share his vulnerability. He didn't have to say another word. When he spoke about himself, he was always invariably speaking about me.

'I have no way out,' I whispered. 'If I kill myself, I am nothing more than a coward. If I stay alive, it will probably kill everyone else. I can't win.'

'If you step off that pier, believe me, you will kill everyone else. You may as well take your kids with you.'

'I want to go home,' I said softly.

'I'll take you home now.'

'No. I mean I want to go *home*. My *real* home,' I cried.

'Don't leave before the miracle happens,' he said quietly.

The miracle. I so wanted the miracle to happen. I really did, more than anything else in the world. Why did I want it? I wanted it for the kids. I wanted to be well for them. I wanted them to be free of my affliction. I wanted them to be free from worrying about me. Suddenly I wanted to be alive – just for them. Like the high-pitched snapping of a camera reaching the end of a roll, the 'suicidal psalm' ran out of film.

In that moment, I switched from self-obsession to something else. I no longer wanted for me. I understood that my life was a vast production, and the cast was the world I inhabited.

'What if the miracle has already passed me by?'

'But, sweetheart, can't you see? It's happening right now,' he said, smiling.

My feet gingerly stepped back from the edge. Charlie gripped my arms, locking them with his. The tears tumbled forth with no warning. My shoulders heaved with the ferocity of their pent-up imprisonment; like escaped convicts, my gut-wrenching sobs spilled over.

Charlie rocked me.

'You're going to be OK. I don't know much, but I do know you'll be OK,' he said.

The mournful weeping went on for an age. I seemed to be unleashing a lifetime of misery. It felt like the exorcism of a thousand generations and, when I was done, there was nothing left but me.

'Charlie, I owe you an apology. I once accused you of not being a friend. I was wrong. You're more than that. I think you're my guardian angel.'

'A friend is someone who comes in when the world goes out. Maybe friends are guardian angels too.'

'Well, if you're mine, I should be dead by now.'

'Yeah, you're right. If I'm a guardian angel, then the whole world is fucked.'

We both laughed.

'Tell you what,' he said. 'If things don't improve soon, I promise you, I will find a gun and shoot you myself. How's that?'

'It's a deal.'

'Do you get that?'

'Get what?'

'That smell.'

'What smell?'

'The chipper. Mmmm. Fish and chips. Fancy a fresh cod?'

7

They say a breakdown is, in fact, a breakthrough. This theory must hold some weight, because the miracle did happen slowly. So slowly, it almost eluded me, but that is the nature of miracles. They creep up on you and are happening before you can say 'Medjugorje is a crock of shit and Lourdes is just the name of Madonna's daughter.'

Not long after my brush with suicide, my life began to change. I had always viewed miracles as acts of providence visited only upon the most holy. But I have learned that if you're even slightly open to the concept, they can occur to just about anyone. Miracles are soft and tenuous, often working over a period of time. Hence their mysterious machinations tend to escape us, and we don't appreciate them for the truly divine orchestrations they are.

I continued to turn up for the 'big show' every day. This was my saving grace. I still believe it is the only requirement necessary for taking part in the great, cosmic waltz. I put my implicit trust in a God of my understanding, and I discovered that waltzing was not as difficult as I had thought.

I knew I had not been brought to such a place to be let down. I knew I had not been dragged through the recovery process to be given a bum deal. God would not short-change me. All my needs had been met so far. I hadn't acquired my insatiable wants, but then again, no one had promised I would. I knew life had infinitely improved, and somewhere deep inside I had a sneaking suspicion that it could be even better.

By now Charlie had adopted a new member into his family: a dilapidated, white Ford Cortina. The Cortina was a step up the ladder for Charlie, a real bargain at a whopping £49. Charlie failed to notice that the jalopy was virtually uninhabitable. None of the windows wound up or down, the car seats were sprouting springs, and the gear stick (a thin piece of metal with a red knob on the top) had a habit of immobilising itself. The tyres were threadbare, and the registration plate hung precariously by a piece of string. But in the defects ratio, the 'horn that didn't hoot' took first prize.

Charlie's resourcefulness proved ingenious. He broke the driver's window in and used his arm to make hand signals. He took to wearing one glove only, and could only ever drive with his right hand flapping about on the outside. He infuriated other law-abiding drivers on the road, thrashing his arm about randomly. If he was turning left, he wiggled his arm; if he was turning right, he wiggled his arm; if he was stopping, he wiggled his arm. As far as he was concerned, he was the epitome of road etiquette.

'What's your fucking problem, pal?' he'd curse, half his torso hanging over the car door. Collision should have been imminent. But like Mr McGoo, Charlie miraculously managed to evade accident after accident. How many he caused is another story. We christened the Ford Cortina 'the white piece of shite' and held a private christening ceremony before it officially hit the road. We lit candles and stuck a broken pair of rosary beads on to the sun visor. Charlie said the prayers.

'Dear God. Please bless the white piece of shite and keep safe all who sail in her. Amen. PS, if you can fix the windows, that would be deadly. Amen again.' We concluded with takeaway coffee, muffins and several cans of air freshener. The rosary beads whacked me in the face as we set off on our way to a meeting. I felt protected and terrified, both at the same time.

'Listen to that engine. What a lovely hum,' Charlie said proudly. 'Chitty chitty bang bang, eh?'

'Erm, yeah, Mr Potts,' I replied, while the rosary beads

gashed my forehead and the springs in the seat tore the arse out of my jeans. An incensed BMW honked loudly as Charlie turned a corner.

'FTWs,' he barked out the window.

'FTWs?'

'Fucking time wasters.'

Life was *so* good.

I had much to be thankful for, and I had Charlie to thank for it all. I wanted to show my appreciation in a special way, but was stymied when it came to getting the quintessential thank-you gift. Eventually, I came up with the perfect means of expressing my gratitude. I had managed to decode all his handwritten ditties, and slowly turned them into the poems they were destined to be. I went to a local stationer and had all the pages bound. It felt like a meagre offering but I hadn't the money to buy him something better. I was quite excited about giving it to him. I had gift-wrapped it, signed the inside, dated, addressed and entitled each poem. The binding was brown leather, with his name inscribed on the cover.

One Saturday morning, Charlie was doing his customary car boot sale stint. I decided to surprise him with the gift. When I caught up with him, he was sitting in the driver's seat, feet up on the dashboard, plastic cup in hand, egg sandwich and pouch of tobacco perched on the steering wheel.

'I still can't believe you actually paid money for this,' I shouted in the smashed window.

'It's as good as new. Has a brand new—'

'Engine . . . I know.' I climbed in the back and made a space for myself amongst the broken washing-machine parts, vacuum-cleaner tubes and dismantled toasters.

'Hey, watch the valuables, will ya?' Charlie eyeballed me through the rearview mirror.

I pulled a rubber dog bone from underneath my thigh and stared at it, then back at him in the mirror.

'What? It once belonged to Lassie. It's the genuine article,' he said solemnly. I pushed it aside, along with a pair of blunt shears, a bowl of plastic fruit, and a St Martin de Porres statue: someone had painted his toenails pink and pierced his left ear.

'Jesus, it stinks in here.'

'It's the egg sandwiches. Here, have a cup of tea.' He handed me a plastic beaker.

'I brought something for you,' I said.

'Is it of any value?'

'That all depends.'

'Depends on what? I have to earn a shilling, you know.'

'It's not of any monetary value, if that's what you mean.

Well, maybe not yet,' I smiled, handing him the parcel.

Charlie peeled back the wrapping paper, and went silent when he saw what it was. He held the bound poems in both hands, brought it to his nose and sniffed the pungent leather. He opened it and read the inscription, then slowly flicked from one page to the next.

'Well?' I said.

'This is my work?'

'It sure is. Do you like it? It even has your name inscribed on the front.'

'So it has.' His fingers traced the letters on the front. The shared silence between us was poignant.

'I don't know what to say.'

'"Thank you" will do!'

'Thank you.' He paused, then turned right around. '*Thank . . . you*,' he said more emphatically. 'I am very touched. Very touched indeed.' He dipped his hat protectively over his eyes, shielding a getaway, solitary tear. He cradled the book to his chest, like a newborn infant, a precious jewel. But Charlie's unveiled vulnerability was fleeting.

'I hope you didn't spend any money on this. How much did it cost? You haven't got the money to be doing this kind of thing. How many times do I have to tell you to mind your pennies?'

'It cost very little – only my time.'

For once, Charlie was lost for words.

When the last of the car boot shoppers had left the market, we gathered up the remaining bits and bobs of the sales stock and drove to the northside to catch an evening meeting. We had made an extra bit of money that day, so we decided after the meeting to drift into Abrakebabra. Charlie was dressed in his Frank Sinatra best: a two-piece brown pinstripe suit, lemon shirt, blue tie, cowboy boots and a grey trilby with white felt around the base.

A few wilting dandelions sat in a small, thin glass on the table. He plucked one from its obscurity and stuck it in the rim of his hat.

'You look like a complete Worzel Gummidge.'

'I have a reputation to keep up.'

I poked at a carton of cold chips while Charlie rolled a cigarette. He lit up, tipped his hat forward and started to swirl his coffee.

'I have to say, that was a really powerful meeting just there.'

'Yeah, it's amazing, isn't it? No matter what mood you're in, it lifts you.'

'Yup. Going to a meeting is a bit like going to an orgy. I always come out feeling better, and I never know who to thank.'

I sniggered.

'So what's been happening?'

'Nothing much.'

'How is work?'

'Work is fine. I'm up for a permanent job. Chances are I will get it too.'

'Humph.'

'Kids are good, too. Jason got an A in his English test. Teacher says he's coming on great. I finally got him the guitar he wanted. He plays it all day and, get this, at night he takes it into the bed and sleeps with it.'

'Be grateful. There are worse things he could be sleeping with.'

'Did you have to say that?'

'I guess not.'

'Reece is born to be on the stage. I'm thinking of enrolling her in drama classes.'

'Drama classes? After what she did to your house, I think bulldozing lessons would be much more suitable. Why don't you just buy her a wrecking ball?'

'Life is peachy. It can't get any better.'

'Guess what?' Charlie fiddled with the dandelion in his hat 'It *does*.'

Just then, the door was flung open violently, and there was a rush of air. The type that had a distinct tinge of menace in its tail. A tall, emaciated-looking young man raced in. Charlie had his back to him, but I could see him full on. He stood for a few seconds, then promptly jumped the serving counter and lunged at the assistant. It all happened so quickly, it didn't really dawn on me what was going on. I felt Charlie's cowboy boot kick my shoe underneath the table. His eyes met mine, his expression stoic and serious, and then I understood that we were in the middle of a raid.

Charlie's eyes spoke quite clearly to me: don't move an inch, they begged.

The young man looked deranged. From the corner of my eye, I could see his long matted hair. I could smell his desperation, too. I was terrified. My primary concern was my handbag. I had left it open in full view on the table in front of me. I dipped my eyes towards it and Charlie picked up my signal immediately. The youth was shouting and roaring at the top of his voice for the assistant to hand over any cash she had. The assistant nervously tried to explain to him that there was no cash held on the premises. It was deposited in a safe in the floor; the safe was time-locked, and could be opened only by the manager. This was the last thing the youth wanted to hear.

Charlie's hands slowly came to rest on the counter while the youth continued to yell at the petrified assistant. During this altercation, Charlie whipped my bag off the table and slid it down between his feet. He gave me a quick wink and kicked my shoe gently.

'Hey you!' the youth screamed at him.

I'm sure my face turned as ashen as Charlie's hat.

Charlie turned his head to face the youth. Slowly, he tipped his hat backwards and stared him right between the eyes.

'What the fuck are you doing?' the youth yelled.

Please don't answer. This is no time to be a hero! I implored Charlie with my petrified pupils.

The youth stood next to me, glaring at Charlie. His jaws were sunken craters and his dirty clothes clung to his bony frame. His height only accentuated his gaunt, skeletal figure.

'Give me the bag,' he demanded.

Charlie didn't budge.

'I said give me the fucking bag or I'll stick this in your fucking gut.'

He pulled out a small knife from his back pocket and wielded it menacingly in front of Charlie's face, but this violent gesture did not faze Charlie.

Give him the fucking bag! I pleaded with Charlie with my wide eyes.

Charlie slowly slipped his hand inside his jacket and pulled out his wallet. He handed it calmly to the youth, who snatched it greedily.

'No bag,' Charlie said softly. 'Touch the bag and I'll see to it that every cop on the northside is out looking for you. I never forget a face. Never.'

The youth looked momentarily dazed. He took a long look at the wallet in his hand. I could hear the addiction speaking to him. He had the wallet. He wasn't going to waste any more time. He hadn't the foresight to consider that he would need more cash later. All that mattered was getting the next fix, and he needed that fix *now*.

The rest of the customers sat still and silent. No one dared move or speak. The assistant stood perfectly motionless, her hand poised on the alarm, her ghostly face filled with trepidation, reflecting back at us through the mirror.

The youth ran. He was gone so quickly, it was hard to believe anything had happened at all. I realised that my knuckles had gone pure white. After what felt like hours, Charlie stood up and walked to the door.

'The coast is clear,' he reassured the assistant, who then pushed the alarm bell with all her might. The other customers leapt up and ran. I was still rooted to the spot. The assistant wavered unsteadily on her feet. I was sure she was going to collapse.

'Quick, a glass of water,' Charlie said to me.

I went over to the counter and held tight on to the poor assistant, who was beginning to look the worse for wear. I brought the remains of my Coke and held it against her lips.

'That's the fourth time this week,' she gasped.

'Christ.'

'Yeah. Local guy. Cops know him well.'

'Well, they'll be along soon I expect,' Charlie put in, patting the girl on the back and making her sit down. 'No need to worry any more. He's well gone by now. Wanker.' Charlie burst into a terrible coughing fit. It was a really bad attack. He pressed his hands down on the countertop as he fought for air.

'You should take a seat yourself,' I suggested. He waved me off angrily. There was no talking to him.

We waited for the Gardaí to come. It was quite a long wait. They drove up outside some twenty-five minutes later. One thing was instantly obvious. They weren't in any rush to solve 'The Great Abrakebabra Robbery'.

'Let me guess,' the bigger detective said, perusing the immediate surroundings. 'Our local hero, Colin the heroin addict, causing trouble again?'

The assistant nodded in accord. 'Fourth time this week.'

'Jesus. This guy is such an idiot. He knows quite well there's no cash on the premises, yet he still comes in here hoping there might be,' the second Garda joked. The other one laughed out loud. This incensed the assistant.

'Look, lads, I know it's great gas and all, but what I can't understand is if you know who this guy is and where he lives, why can't you arrest the little fucker? My nerves are shattered going through this over and over. I shouldn't have to deal with thugs like him. One of these days he's going to do as he threatens, and someone will get hurt. Chances are, it's going to be me.'

Charlie and I nodded.

'Who are these two?' the cop asked.

'Witnesses,' the assistant sighed. 'For what they're fucking worth,' she added sarcastically.

'Well, I have good news for you. We caught the little shite a hundred yards up the road.'

'What?' we all said in unison.

'Yup. He's handcuffed in the back of the van. That's why we were so late getting here. Anyone by the name of Charlie Gallagher here? We found your wallet.'

'Well, thank Christ for small mercies,' I said, crossing myself.

'Yeah, but for how long will he be off the streets this time?' the assistant asked, a mixture of relief and new anxiety washing over her expression.

'He's going down for good this time.'

'How can you be so sure?'

'We have him lock, stock and barrel. Fucking eejit robbed this old car, a heap of crap from outside. Sure, he only got ten yards up the road with it and the engine clapped out. No petrol in the thing! What kind of gobshite thinks that yoke is roadworthy is beyond me. A scrap merchant wouldn't pay you to take it.'

Charlie turned to face me, his grin as wide as the San Francisco Bridge. He threw his arms up in the air and shrugged: 'Did I not say that life would get even better?'

I cracked up.

It didn't occur to me till years later what Charlie had really done that day. First of all, he had defended me. Secondly, he had put his life in danger for the sake of a lousy cheap plastic handbag, simply because it was mine. Thirdly, he had lost his 'great love' (the car), and been willing to sacrifice his own wallet. And all of it was done in my honour. He never once complained about any of it either. Now that was the stuff of a *real* James Bond.

The 'white piece of shite' was towed away by the Gardaí, never to be seen again. Charlie claimed on his insurance. He had his heart set on a mustard-coloured Fiat 127, a horrible object that resembled a tin box of Cadburys Roses on four rubber tubes. Just to make sure the ignition did actually turn on and it had sufficient petrol in it to get us home, I arranged to meet him at the makeshift garage on Summerhill where Charlie was going to buy it. I looked over the vile Fiat while waiting for Charlie to arrive. Only he never did.

I spent an hour walking back and forth to a public phone box and calling his home. I could only get the answering machine. After several more failed attempts, his daughter eventually answered the phone.

'Hiya, Mary, it's Cath. Charlie never turned up to pick up the new car. I'm a bit worried. He wouldn't miss this for the Pope. Do you know where he's at? Did he get delayed?'

Charlie's daughter paused. I could hear her trying to disguise her muffled sobs.

'Don't you know? He was admitted to Beaumont Hospital late last night.'

8

I went straight to the hospital. The journey had provided me with the opportunity to work through various scenarios. My imagination was sparked and, like an Australian bushfire, it raged uncontrollably. I wondered what was wrong with Charlie. A catalogue of reasons for his hospitalisation raced through my mind. By the time I got there, I had calmed myself enough to conjure a feigned composure. No matter what the problem was, he didn't need me arriving at the height of hysteria.

Charlie had been settled in a private room on the second floor. I found him sitting upright in bed, chatting and smiling with a small Filipino nurse.

'Oh, such a funny man!' She waved her hand at me, leaving the room in convulsions.

'Tell me about it,' I smirked.

'It's the rotten rip,' he grunted.

'What the hell are you doing here?'

'How the fuck should I know? I was hoping you'd be able to tell me.'

'Where's the family?'

'Probably at the undertakers. I hope they don't buy one of those gaudy coffins. You know, with elaborate scenes of the Last Supper on the sides.'

'Charlie, calm down. I don't think we're talking last rites yet.'

'The family made me come in. They know I hate hospitals.'

'I know you do, too, but you must be here for some good reason.'

'You tell me. I'm all out of conspiracy theories.'

'Charlie, you need a good looking-over. You've been ill for months.'

'I have been sitting here imagining my deathbed scene. You know, the family all standing around me, sobbing uncontrollably, racked with unremitting guilt, begging for my forgiveness – only I'll die before I can give it to them, just to spite the bastards.'

'That's no way to talk about your loved ones. They are concerned for your health.'

'I told the nurse there's nothing wrong with me, and this is all a fuss about nothing. I have some kind of rare flu they can't figure out.' He coughed wearily.

'Of course it's a *rare* flu – some as-yet-undiscovered tropical strain. Can you not just have an ordinary flu like everyone else?' I sat on the edge of the bed and sighed.

He scowled and frowned, deepening the creases on his forehead. He was very angry. In an instant I knew what was bothering him. The hat was off. He couldn't wear a hat in a hospital bed. So he was effectively naked. He had nowhere to hide. Charlie rubbed his bald patch protectively and eyed me suspiciously. I pretended not to notice.

'Do you want me to leave?' I asked softly.

'I'm not sick.'

'OK, OK. If you say so.'

'Humph.'

'This is routine stuff, Charlie. People come in and out of hospital all the time. They probably just want to run some tests.'

'Blah blah.'

'You'll be in here a couple of days max.'

'Humph.'

'Have you eaten anything?'

'How could I? The food is so bad, the United Nations sent it back. A Third World country wouldn't eat it.'

'What did you expect: Jamie Oliver? It's a public hospital

and the staff are always extremely busy. I imagine à la carte menus are relatively low on their priority list.'

'No shit? I bet every patient who came in here had a clean bill of health to start out with. That is before they ate. That's why there's no available beds. It's a fucking food-poisoning epidemic.'

'You have to eat.'

'Stop mammying me. I hate that. Next thing, you'll want to know did I do a shite. That's all the nurses keep asking me. They seem unhealthily obsessed with the movement of my bowels. They keep giving me laxatives. I'm sure I'm going to give birth to a child through my arse any minute now.'

I tried to keep a straight face.

'I keep telling everyone that I have the flu, some viral thinga-majig. Wouldn't you think with all their training in those foreign lands they'd know what it is? I could have the bubonic plague.'

'I wouldn't worry unduly. The last case of bubonic plague in Europe was in the eighteenth century.'

'Maybe I have a new strain of mad cow disease? Why is it called mad cow disease anyway? It's very offensive to the cows. If I were a cow, I'd be highly insulted. Why not call it something more humane. Like mentally challenged cow disease?'

'Have you seen a doctor yet? Have they said anything about tests?'

'Who cares what they said? If they can't figure out the cows, what fucking chance have I got?'

'What would you tell me now if the roles were reversed? You would tell me to co-operate and get on with it, wouldn't you?'

'Ah Jaysus,' he sighed.

'It's true,' I said.

'You're loving this, ya rotten rip.'

'Truly, I'm not.'

'I will do what the bastards tell me, but I'm not stopping smoking. Just so you know.'

'Did I tell you to stop smoking?'

He reached under the mattress, pulled out a pouch of tobacco and held it up.

'Did I tell you I ain't stopping?'

The fact that he was actually in the bed, in his pyjamas, in a hospital, was a miracle in itself. One thing I was certain of: I bet he rebelled, kicking and bucking every step of the way.

Granted, he had his pyjama buttons done up wrong. His little bit of defiance. He yanked back the covers and scuttled over to the small window on the left-hand side of the room. He pushed open the window, lit up and puffed for Ireland.

'Em, Charlie, I don't think you're allowed to smoke in hospital,' I chanced gently.

'Watch my lips,' he said childishly, sucking on the cigarette like a lollipop, breathing in the smoke and exhaling it out of the tiny porthole window. He revelled in this display of insubordination, and I wasn't going to steal his thunder.

'Come back to your bed before the nurse returns and blames me for your insolence. I have some good news for you.'

He bumbled over to the bed, and climbed in obediently. I pulled the covers up over him, straightened them, tucked them in at the sides, and plumped up his pillows.

'There. Comfortable?'

'Fucking dandy.'

I took a brown paper bag from my handbag and plonked it on his lap.

'A pressie? For me?' His face lit up as he tore at the bag, then his face dropped.

'Fruit?'

'It's healthy.'

'Fucking fruit?'

I placed the large bottle of Lucozade on the bedside locker.

'You *are* in hospital.'

'Fruit? Lucozade? Why do people bring fruit in to patients in hospitals? Why not a Big Mac or a nice fat cigar? Are you deliberately trying to knock me off? If you are, you'd better make sure you get the head first.'

'It's good for you.'

'Me teeth can't handle apples. You know that. You did it on purpose.'

'Charlie.'

'Can't you go and get me some ice cream from the shop? I swear your conscience will feel better if you do me a good turn. You see, even now, I'm thinking of your mental health. The constant thought of others. It stops you thinking about yourself. What the hell have I been teaching you all these years?'

'I said no.'

'Have you no pity for an old man?'

'Since when are you old?'

'That's it. I want to see a Garda and make an official statement. I want people to know the truth before I pop my clogs. I can already see the coroner's report in my mind's eye. Cause of death: chronic neglect. You're trying to kill me.'

'If I murdered you now, I would have nothing to look forward to.'

Charlie held the torn brown paper bag up in the air. He looked at me with desperate eyes.

'Jaysus. Don't tell me this was the good news?'

I steadied myself on the side of the bed so that I was staring straight at him. I was about to tell him about the Fiat, which I had christened 'the custard crock', but the nurse burst in the door, a brusque breeze following her. Her efficient air charged the room.

'Do I smell smoke?' she said, looking at him sternly.

'It's probably yourself you're smelling. I've seen you at the bus stop at the entrance to the hospital.' Charlie gave her a wide grin. 'Smoke enough cigarettes to ignite a bonfire, don't ya?' Charlie's hand gently crept to the underside of the mattress, where he reassuringly patted his hidden treasure.

'Mr Gallagher, there are strict no-smoking rules in this hospital, and you must adhere to them. If you don't, we shall have to ask you to leave.' The nurse gave him a look that would wither a Valentine's Day bouquet.

'No need to ask. Where's me clothes?'

'Oh, please. Don't play right into his hands!' I begged her.

'I'm sorry. Rules are rules,' she nodded at me.

'She's right. Rules are rules. I broke them, and now I deserve to be punished. Where's me bag, and I'll be on my way.' Charlie fumbled with the covers, making to get up.

'Not so fast.' The nurse pushed him back down.

'See, she's trying to hold me hostage! I want to see the head nurse,' Charlie demanded petulantly.

'You're looking at her, mister.'

'Oh. You've a fine head of hair on ya. Did anyone ever tell you that?'

The head nurse grinned.

'Are you a relative?' she asked me, as she began setting up a blood-pressure machine.

'A friend,' I answered.

'I'm not sick,' he growled under his breath.

'Remain still.' She wrapped the blood-pressure band around his arm and started to pump.

'Let me guess: 1,000 over 20? See, not a bother on me,' Charlie barked.

'Stop jigging about or I'll glue your arse to the bed.'

'I'm not sick,' he continued to object.

'As stubborn as a garden weed.' The nurse tut-tutted. She slipped her hand expertly under the mattress and confiscated the pouch of tobacco.

'What's this?' she asked.

'She put it there,' Charlie said, pointing straight at me.

'Along with the fruit and the Lucozade?'

'As sure as God is my judge, I don't know how that got there.'

'Is there anything else under there that I should know about? A few bottles of whiskey? Some kilos of cocaine?' She leaned right up against Charlie's face.

'Nothing. Unless you consider the *Irish Times* to be hard-core porn. Or a Vicks nasal spray to be a dangerous narcotic.'

'Your family are outside waiting to see you.'

'I don't want to see them,' Charlie said sulkily.

'That's very rude, Mr Gallagher.'

'You keep telling me I'm sick. If I'm sick, then I'm entitled to be rude. Tell them I'm in a coma.'

'Charlie, you are being difficult, childish, self-centred and impossible,' I intervened.

'And the problem is?'

'I'll pray for you,' the nurse grinned.

'No need – you can have me any time you like.'

The nurse chuckled. As soon as she had closed the door, I turned to Charlie and looked him straight in the eye.

'We need to talk seriously.'

'I know.'

'You have to stop smoking.'

'I will.'

'Like right now, Charlie. Not tomorrow.'

He slowly sat up in the bed and whipped a half-puffed ciga-rette from out of his top pyjama pocket.

'Do bears shit in the woods?'

Outside the room, Charlie's family had gathered. They hud-dled in a group, whispering. I felt bad about having been in the room before them.

'Cathy?' One of his children called me over.

'Look, I'm so sorry,' I said. 'I know I had no business coming in like this, unannounced. I wasn't thinking. You're family. I shouldn't be here. Forgive my insensitivity.'

'It's OK.' She smiled at me.

'How long do you think he'll be in here? What exactly are they doing anyway – some chest x-rays? If so, it's about bloody time. That cough has been getting steadily worse. I kept telling him to go to the doctor, but he refused point blank.'

'Don't you know?' she looked at me quizzically.

'Know what?'

'Dad has lung cancer, Cathy.'

I fled the hospital in a complete state and found myself huddled in the little bus shelter outside the exit, sobbing unashamedly in front of strangers. My hands trembled as I tried to light up a cigarette. The irony was lost on me. There I was lighting up a cigarette and putting it to my lips and breathing its toxins into my lungs, smoking the same poisonous object that was responsible for making my dearest best friend ill. Of course, the cigarette did nothing to allay the fear. Charlie could die. The shock was overwhelming. It felt like I was wearing my skin inside out. I paced along the pavement, wondering what to do, trying to think what Charlie would expect of me in this situation. What would he have me do? What would he have me think?

No one paid the slightest attention to my deranged rhetoric. I emoted at will, telling myself over and over that he would fight this disease as valiantly as he had done his alcoholism. This was not a time to enter into a pessimistic frame of mind. That's not what he would want me to do. In fact, he would expect me to be strong and positive.

I had found faith in a higher power again, thanks to Charlie. It was time to put that faith into practice. More than ever, I knew I needed to turn the whole thing over to God. I had to have implicit and unhesitating conviction in my heart that God's help, coupled with Charlie's unwavering will, would be enough to get him through. He would apply himself to this battle with the same vigour and self-assurance that he had done before. There was no room for doubt.

I returned to the hospital – but not to Charlie. I took the long corridor all the way down to the small, antiquated hospital chapel, blinking back my tears. At the top of the chapel, I knelt down. A picture of the Sacred Heart was on the wall in front of me.

'*Sacred Heart of Jesus, I place all my trust in thee,*' it read.

'Right,' I said aloud. 'I'm in.'

And I started praying. I started praying hard.

9

Recovery can be a bastard; recovery can be the greatest high you'll ever experience. It all depends on what head space you're in on the day. The good news is, you get your feelings back. The bad news is, you get your feelings back. It's a catch-22.

The word 'balance' comes hard to any recovering alcoholic. To most, it is a word that doesn't exist in the Oxford dictionary, let alone their vocabulary. As a recovering addict, I was no different to others in this regard, often describing myself as being 'in the depths of recovery'. That summed it all up. To suggest I plunged into a deep despair over the news of Charlie's cancer is an understatement. I was devastated.

What recovery did provide me with, though, were the skills to keep my pain at bay. It kind of hovered about me, like some invisible computer virus. I wasn't letting it get into the hard drive. I was aware of its presence, and used every antidote available to me. All the meetings I had attended began to pay off, like deposits in a bank account; it was time to draw on them to safeguard myself. Every meeting had acted like an insurance policy. That dreaded rainy day had arrived, and it was time to cash it in. I reverted to Charlie's advice when I had initially stopped drinking: I would deal with his cancer and my own emotional squalls 'one day at a time'.

I took to visiting Charlie daily. It wasn't a formal arrangement; I just did it automatically. Mostly I sat and watched as nurses and doctors filed in and out of his room. Charts were written up. A battery of tests were undertaken. Whispered conversations took place outside the door. Flowers and cards and balloons arrived, filling the room with hope and good cheer. So did lots of visitors. Charlie became very quiet. Not sullen, just conservatively withdrawn. He seemed to retreat to some private place within himself. It was an exclusive journey, and I was not willing to push him to share it with me. I had no notion of what it felt like to be told you had cancer, or how one would attempt to come to terms with such a disclosure.

By the fourth day, he was talking again, and walking around the corridors with the help of a cane. His face was like thunder as he banged the stick on the ground.

I caught up with him and called from behind.

'Charlie?'

'Humph.'

'Did they give you a cane?'

'Well, what do you think this is – a fucking fishing rod?'

'At least you can move around.'

'I can move around without it. I'm just humouring the bastards.'

Despite his best efforts, I could see that each step was a great strain on his failing lungs. I moved in beside him, timing my paces, careful not to walk too fast, so he wouldn't think he was being too slow. I thought about slipping my arm into his so he would have some extra support, but I didn't want him to feel helpless. I let him fumble onwards, alone.

'How are you feeling today?'

'We all know how I am.'

'Have you had any visitors?'

'Yes. I've had relatives I haven't seen in thirty years. Cousins I never knew existed. All sniffing around waiting for me to keel over.'

'They're just being kind,' I offered.

'Yeah? The crack cocaine dealer from Number 67 dropped in. Probably thought I was on the morphine patches. Do they think I stock them in me fucking bedside locker?'

I was a bit taken aback. Not by the anger, but by the fact that Charlie had any knowledge of morphine.

'I'm sick talking about me. How are you?'

'Never mind me.'

'But we must mind you. Remember, it helps me to focus on something other than myself. Now, give me some peace and tell me how *you* are.'

I was silent for a moment. I didn't think it appropriate to be talking about my own petty problems.

'And think before you answer that one. No lies please. If you lie, I have failed in my job as a sponsor.'

'I'm fine,' I lied.

'Sure. FINE . . . as in Fucked up, Insecure, Neurotic and Emotional?'

'Well, what am I supposed to say?'

'Tell it like it is. That's what I taught you. Say exactly how you feel on the day. Are you paying attention?'

'Yes.'

'Let's start again. How are you *really*?'

'I'm pretty shit.'

'Humph.'

'I feel useless, powerless. I don't know what to say or do.'

'Uh huh.'

'I don't know what you need from me.'

'Hah!'

'I don't know why you think that's funny.'

'Maybe I need something from *you*?'

'That never entered my head.'

'Of course not. You're an alcoholic.'

I felt smaller than a mouse dropping. I must have looked like one, too.

'Where's your sense of humour gone? That was a joke, ya rotten rip.'

'Oh, right.'

We had reached his private room, and as I sat on the bed, he rummaged around. A small TV and video player had been installed in the corner.

'Hey, you have a telly?'

'Yeah, but it doesn't work.' Charlie took two remotes from his locker and started to pound the two of them at the same time. He looked like Jack Palance duelling in the old western *Shane*. The front of the video player opened and closed, opened and closed.

'Damn batteries.'

'Give me them,' I said, relieving him of the remotes. I eventually got the television going.

'Look, it's *Oprah*,' I said. 'She's got that famous author on.'

Charlie squinted at the telly.

'How the fuck did *he* get on *Oprah*? He can't write shit. I've read better plots in Glasnevin Cemetery.'

'Personal assistants. Hairdressers. Stylists. He's got dollar wads coming out of his fucking hole. Laughing all the way to his stretch limo.'

'That reminds me. The car?' he said.

'What car?'

'The Fiat?'

'Oh. That car. Don't be overly concerned. I don't think anyone in their right mind would buy it.'

'A bargain if I ever saw one. I should have put a deposit on it the minute I saw it.'

'I suppose you're right; which is why I put a deposit on it myself. Just in case.'

'You did?' Charlie put his head down. I wasn't sure if I had upset him or made him happy.

'I see you're writing?' I changed the subject. Bits of crumpled-up paper lay strewn about the bed and the floor. I was also pleasantly pleased to see the leather-bound book of poems that I had given him sitting on the bedside locker.

'My solicitor. She has me writing more letters than St Paul wrote to the Corinthians.'

I felt my tummy do a double somersault. I didn't want to hear anything pertaining to 'legal' matters.

'I'm also doing some written work with an AA newcomer.'

'What?'

'You heard me.'

'By post?'

'Yup. What's wrong with that?'

I was gobsmacked that anyone who had just been diagnosed with cancer could be still thinking of other people.

'Are you sure you're up for that?' I asked tentatively.

'Life goes on,' he said, grabbing my arm. We went back out into the corridors and walked to the small coffee shop near the entrance. Charlie leaned his nose against the window. Strictly speaking, he wasn't supposed to go in there, but strictly speaking didn't count for much any more.

'I smell coffee. Mmmm,' he said, closing his eyes and breathing in the aroma. I pushed him through the coffee-shop door, walked to the counter and bought two coffees and two plates of chips.

'I didn't do this, right?' I said as I sat down opposite him and arranged our food.

'Do what?' he said innocently, a small grin appearing on his smug face.

'I see you got your hat back.'

'I can't go walking in the corridors bare-headed; it gets the nurses too excited.'

I smiled.

'I try to wear a different one every day. I know it looks odd with a pair of pyjamas, but they ain't taking my dignity as well as everything else.'

I wondered what the 'everything else' was.

'I brought you some books. Thrillers. I hope you like them. It was either thrillers or romantic Barbara Cartland shit. That's all they had in the shop. I know you want to survive this, so I chose the thrillers.'

'Powerlessness.'

'I don't know how these guys concoct such elaborate story-lines. Jesus, I couldn't be arsed working them out.'

'You know, powerlessness is power in its purest form.'

'Who cares anyway if Joe shot Mary's aunt's half-cousin's sister-in-law in the end? They're all the same. Like the mushy romantic novels. There are always "heaving bosoms", "pert nipples" and "firm thighs", not to mention "thrusting members". There's a fierce amount of them. And have you noticed everything seems to be "engorged"? You can't have a Mills and Boon without the word "engorged".'

'When you're powerless and you really know it, deep in your heart, you couldn't be in a better place.'

'And have you ever wondered why all the women have green, almond-shaped eyes and long, chestnut hair that falls in loose tresses about their milky-skinned shoulders? They always seem to love horse-riding too. Just as well though. Every heroine seems to have to endure his overpowering manhood breaking her maidenhead every ten minutes. You'd be fucking knackered just reading about it.'

'It feels uncomfortable. It feels strange. It feels like you're lost, but actually being powerless gives you wonderful autonomy.'

'Autonomy?'

'It means independence, self-sufficiency.'

'You mean "engorged"? No, I think it means swollen.'

'Will you listen?' he barked at the top his voice. 'I am talking about powerlessness.'

'Well, I'm sorry, but I don't feel any sense of independence watching you being ill.'

'Are you angry?' He dipped his hat downwards and slowly stirred his coffee.

'Of course I'm fucking angry,' I spat.

'Good. That's all normal.' Swirl, swirl.

'Charlie, I don't think—'

'I'm talking now. You shut your mouth.'

I shut my mouth.

'There's not going to be a right time. There's not going to be a perfect moment, a peaceful place becoming available where we can all say what we need to say to each other. This is reality. We are not Cathy and Heathcliff out on the moors. This is not a novel.'

'Charlie, please, we don't need to go there. You'll be out soon enough. Everything is fine. You'll be back on your feet in no time.'

He slammed his cup of coffee back on the saucer. Everyone in the restaurant paused.

I bit my lip.

'There's work to be done, and I need your help with it.'

I didn't want to hear any of this. I still wasn't ready.

'I don't know what you're talking about,' I answered defensively.

'I need you,' he said quietly. His eyes locked with mine, and I couldn't steal them away. What was not said in that moment will stay with me for ever. It felt like someone had opened the top of my head and poured a jug of love inside me. I was warmed like a pot of tea, safe inside its woollen cosy.

'First things first.' He cleared his throat.

'Anything you want.'

'I need a fag.'

I frowned.

'You said anything you want?' he smiled.

We shuffled out the doors of the coffee shop to the front

entrance. I knew I was breaking the hospital rules, but I didn't care any more. I was going to do whatever Charlie asked. If the roles had been reversed, I know he would have done exactly the same for me. We sat in the bus shelter, him with his flimsy nightgown, half-hanging off his shoulder, leaning against the cane. Me beside him, rolling him cigarettes and putting them in an old cigarette carton for later. We chain-smoked, not saying much. I endured the filthy looks from unimpressed civilians.

'Hospitals always remind me of treatment centres,' Charlie said.

'Were you in a treatment centre?'

'Once.'

'Oh?'

'I got evicted.'

'Why? What did you do?'

'I wouldn't give a urine sample.'

'You must have done something worse than that.'

'I wouldn't give a urine sample in the bottle. I pissed into a milk carton instead.'

'Oh, Charlie.'

'In the old days, the only way nurses had of knowing whether you'd been abstinent or not was to taste the urine and see if there was any alcohol in it.'

'Jaysus. No wonder they were short-staffed.'

'Humph.'

'The powerlessness thing?'

'Yeah. It's a tough one.'

'I don't understand how you can be so calm.'

'If I was worked up to a pitch, would it change anything?'

'I guess not.'

'That's what's wrong with people today. This delusion they live in that they can actually change things.'

'But people can change.'

'Oh sure, *people* can change. Anyone can decide to change themselves. I meant that they can't change life, other people, et cetera. Life happens no matter what. It's how you deal with it. It's what attitude you're going to take towards your circumstances. Now, you *do* have power over that, for sure. You can take a shitty attitude or you can take a positive attitude. But life? Hey, no one has been able to stop it yet. But by taking action and changing ourselves, we can influence others, sometimes quite powerfully.'

'Mmmm.'

'Look at your kids, for instance. How do you think they might be now, if you hadn't stopped drinking? Are they the better for it?'

'Yes, definitely.'

'When you stopped drinking, had you it in mind that you were going to change them?'

'No.'

'See my point?'

'Yeah. My stability has given them stability.'

'That's it,' he nodded, happy that I was understanding.

'In that moment, when you admitted you were powerless over alcohol and you surrendered, what happened?'

I thought about it for a minute.

'I got strength.'

'Isn't it ironic that when you were at your weakest, this strength came into your life?'

'I never looked at it like that.'

'Look at all these people,' Charlie said, letting out a big sigh. I looked. Throngs of people rushed past, all going somewhere, their faces filled with direction and purpose.

'People use up so much energy, effort and willpower trying to escape life. They're either busy trying to live someone else's, or wasting their efforts on running away from their own. If every individual put even a quarter of that energy into trying to accept their life, deal with it, and leave others alone, what a wonderful world it would be, eh?'

'Yeah, that all sounds great in theory.'

'You have to have a theory before it can become an action.

All actions start in theory.'

'Well, I don't live in theories any more, Charlie.'

'You're missing the point.'

'If this is your roundabout way of telling me I need to be strong, I think I already know that.'

Charlie tipped his hat, dropped his cigarette butt on the ground and drove his slipper into it. It joined the little anthill of other butts that lay at his feet.

'I'm telling you the opposite,' he said reflectively. 'I'm telling you that in your weakness you will find your strength.'

'Is that where you are finding yours?'

I hadn't meant it to come out, but my mouth had never been a muscle that obeyed my commands. My eyes welled up, my stomach was heaving, my throat ached to let out the pain.

'I haven't run my life since 1976. A God of my understanding does that. He's the manager, and he knows what he's doing. I have total faith in him. The day I made the decision that I wasn't in charge any more, my life improved. I gave the job to someone much more qualified and experienced than me. For me to suggest I know better than God is the same as saying I *am* God.'

'But we must turn up and live our lives. We can't just say: "Hey God, can you hang those clothes on the line for me, there's a good man?" We have to make some decisions, and we have to do things.'

'Of course – that's the deal. That's what you call aligning your life with God's will. He does expect me to do certain things. He expects me to do the things I can do. The things I can't do, he does for me, but he never does for me what I can do for myself. How would any of us evolve, or grow, or mature, if God bailed us out of every situation?'

I let this sink in a little.

'Surrender to win, remember?' he said after a long pause.

I suddenly understood that this little conversation was not meant to be a lesson for me. He wasn't trying to teach me any-thing. Charlie was actually sounding out his own strength, and for the first time ever in our relationship, he needed mine. I put my right hand on his and held it there. I feared he would slap it away, or, worse still, take the gesture as patronising. But he remained still, and let me hold his hand. It felt bony and fragile. The two rings he wore (a wedding band and an AA ring) were slightly loose, and they moved back and forth as I gently rubbed against them. I knew he had been losing weight, but I hadn't till that moment acknowledged it inwardly.

Now the reality of the situation hit me. A graphic image of the cancer grew inside my head like some beast – black and insidious. A thick cable, choking and suffocating his lungs. I could see it clearly, as if it were a person, slowly sucking the oxygen from his body and black-balling his vital organs.

I swallowed.

'Say the word, Cathy.'

'Huh?'

'Say the word.'

'What are you on about?'

'Things would be a lot easier for you if you just said the word.'

'What fucking word?'

'The C word.'

'No way.'

'Say it. It's not catching.'

'No. I can't.'

'You can.'

I swallowed hard again.

'Cancer,' I whispered.

'Say it again.'

'Cancer.'

'There, that's not too bad, is it?'

'Cancer,' I repeated, a bit louder now.

'Shout it out,' he ordered.

'Cancer,' I said quite loudly.

'Is that all you can do? Let your fucking lungs go, will ya?'

'*Can-cer!*' I screamed at the top of my voice.

'There. That didn't kill you, did it?'

We both lost it, and fell about the place laughing.

'See? When you vocalise something, it immediately loses its power.'

'Cancer. Cancer. Cancer. Cancer,' I mimicked, using different tones and pitches each time I uttered it.

'Words,' he pondered, 'if internalised, take on a life of their own. And every life has to be followed by a death.'

'Meaning?'

'Don't let words find a home in your soul. Plant them outside of yourself.'

'How?'

'Write them down, my dear.'

I smiled.

'Oh. I almost forgot,' I said, rummaging through my bag excitedly, 'I have a hand-made card from my daughter, and these.' I pulled out two little plastic models of dinosaurs. One was purple, the other green.

'The purple one is supposed to be a man-eater – put him under your pillow. He's fierce and powerful. If you need to kill any enemies, he's the man for the job. I think he's a raptor. The other one is vegetarian. He's a friendly guy. She wants you to have him to play with if you get lonely.'

Charlie's face lit up. He held them in each hand, laughing.

'Kids,' he waxed lyrical. 'Wasn't it some foreign guy who once said: adults never understand anything for themselves, and it is tiresome for kids to be always and forever explaining things to them?'

We made our way back into the hospital, went up in the lift, and walked the corridor to Charlie's room. It was obvious that he had overexerted himself. His face was drawn, the skin beneath his eyes was dark and baggy, and his breathing was laboured. I tucked him in tightly and fluffed up his pillows.

'Read to me,' he asked wearily. I took out my new short story and began to read. By the time I got to the second page, Charlie was asleep. I read him the whole story anyway.

10

It was early September, my favourite time of the year. When the kids go back to school and I get some downtime. It also brought my perfect kind of weather: warm and sunny, not too hot or cold. Autumn announced itself with a typical fanfare, carpeting St Anne's Park in crimson and copper foliage. Having always been a great walker, I took to the pastime more than ever. I spent a great deal of time traipsing the length and breadth of St Anne's Park, kicking up the leaves, watching the squirrels brazenly accumulate the harvest fare, seeing the fat ducks sail towards me in one giant fleet, quacking their way to the pond's edge to feast on my meagre offering of stale bread.

It helped me to focus my thoughts, and did wonders for my muse. I continued with my meetings, my walking, my writing, and my daily visits to Charlie. He had been in hospital for more than three months. There had been talk among family members about moving him to a different hospital, somewhere more comfortable, something akin to a hospice, with specialised staff who were better qualified to deal with his illness.

One beautiful Wednesday morning, I had taken a walk, done some meditating, and completed my household chores earlier than expected. So I decided to go see Charlie. That way, I could fit in an AA meeting later. I arrived on the second floor, walked straight into his room, and stopped dead in my tracks when I realised that Charlie was not in the bed. In fact, the bed had been made up, and all signs of him had been removed. His clothes, his cards, his books, his flowers, every trace of him gone. I panicked and ran to the nurses' station.

'Where is he?' I demanded. The nurses looked from one to the other, solemn and grave.

'Intensive care,' one said eventually.

Fuck, fuck, fuck.

I took the back stairs two at a time, knocking into people, pushing them out of the way. I had to get to Charlie immediately. The hospital was like Grafton Street on a Saturday: droves of people milling about. Where were they all going? Why couldn't they get out of the way? Couldn't they see this was an emergency?

I tried to follow the signs, but there were so many, and I was in such a confused state, I couldn't bring myself to concentrate hard enough and actually read them.

There were no private rooms in the intensive care unit – just a barrage of frenzied activity. I grabbed a passing nurse and she pointed to a bed in the corner. The curtains were firmly pulled around, and I could see quite clearly the outline of figures behind them. There were people in there. I knew the people had to be his family, or doctors, or both. I couldn't bring myself to take another step. All kinds of thoughts invaded my mind. Was I really entitled to go over there and intrude? W hat right had I to go interfering? I was not family. This was the intensive care unit. Charlie must be seriously ill. What if he's taking his last breath right now and I don't get to say goodbye? I could hear low, muffled voices whispering around the bed. Probably family members praying. Why hadn't anyone called me?

I waited. I waited some more. I waited a little more again. I waited maybe for twenty minutes. It was agonising. Eventually, I could take no more. I approached the closed curtains, swallowing hard, shaking uncontrollably. I slipped my hand in the gap of the plastic floral curtain and pushed myself inside. Charlie was sitting upright in the bed, leaning on his hospital tray. His four best male buddies were sitting around on chairs, each of them holding a bunch of cards. There was a big pile of cigarettes in the centre of the tray.

Charlie looked up at me and grinned.

'There's the rotten rip. Fancy a game of poker? I'm up twelve cigarettes so far,' he croaked. Then as an afterthought: 'Hey, what fucker left the kitty shy?'

'What the hell?' I exclaimed.

'Pull up a chair.' One of his friends gestured to an empty seat.

'Will I deal her in, Charlie?' another said nonchalantly.

I wanted to strangle him right there and then. It turned out they were moving him to another private room, which wasn't ready just yet, and the only bed they had in the interim was in intensive care.

Charlie's advancing illness was evident more and more every day. But his sense of humour only improved, and he became quite the character on the second floor. I never understood how he managed to keep his faith. His mind was still as sharp as a butcher's knife, and his wicked wit as infectious as ever. It seemed as if he was happier. He still had his grumpy moments. He got tired easily, and when that happened he simply told everyone to go away and he went asleep. He hardly ate now, but he was still smoking. No one was going to challenge him about that. I caught him several times at the little window in the bedroom having one or two puffs, stabbing the cigarette out and popping it back into his top pyjama pocket. Unfortunately for Charlie, the nurses' station happened to be exactly opposite his window, so every time he stuck his follically challenged head out for a smoke, they caught him red-handed.

Treatment was a word that was forbidden around Charlie. So was 'medication', 'prognosis', 'chemotherapy', 'radiation', and what he referred to as the 'zombie tablets'. He hated the thought of any kind of foreign drug entering his body, even if it meant relief. He didn't believe in any of that 'stuff', but by September, it was obvious to anyone with half a brain that Charlie was in need of some kind of painkiller. I never enquired of the family exactly what pain management Charlie received, but as soon as they started it, he became quieter and slept more.

It was a Friday. A beautiful sunny day. We were experiencing a kind of Indian summer. Temperatures were up, a soft breeze was blowing, and I made my way slowly to the hospital by bus. My mobile phone rang. It was another AA friend of mine.

'What's up?' I asked cheerily.

'He's asking for you,' she said.

Charlie had never once actually asked for me. The bus wouldn't move fast enough. I pondered getting off and walking, or running the rest of the way. Maybe he wanted something in particular? Perhaps he was just feeling exceptionally lonely today? But as I entered his private room, and saw every member of his family sitting around, I knew it was much more serious than I wanted to believe.

Charlie was propped up on several cushions and pillows. One of his children held a small handkerchief under his father's mouth. He seemed to be drooling quite a bit. His face had sunken, exposing the hollow of his cheeks. His body had shrunk to a puny five stone. I could just as easily have turned and walked out. I knew it was Charlie, but he didn't look like Charlie. Except for the startling blue of his eyes, he was unrecognisable.

'He can barely talk,' his daughter said.

In my nervousness, I went to sit on the bed and inadvertently tipped over the tray. All the TV remotes and other objects fell to the floor in one loud clatter.

'That's right,' I heard him say, 'why don't you wreck the fucking place?'

It was a terribly awkward situation. I knew his family didn't want to leave him for one second. I would have felt the same. The room was very small, and people kept filing in and out. Relatives, friends, nurses, doctors. Then out of nowhere, as if God himself had created a little window for us, Charlie's family decided that they needed to talk with his doctor outside the room. Suddenly, we were alone, just us two, face to face. It was our time.

'I asked for pure nicotine. The cow gave me the zombie tablets instead,' Charlie said huskily, each word a terrible effort. He barely lifted his right hand, and motioned towards the drip.

'Oh,' I smiled, getting the joke, but not wanting to find anything funny.

'Now I'm officially a member of the Craft club,' he smiled. I could barely hear him. There was only one thing for it. I climbed up onto the bed and lay down beside him, making sure my ear was beside his mouth. I took both his hands in mine.

'The Craft club – is that what you said?' I asked softly.

'Can't-remember-a-fucking-thing!' He spelt it out slowly.

I started to laugh. I felt so ashamed that I was laughing, but I just couldn't stop. His face lit up momentarily.

'That's my rotten rip,' he said.

'There's nothing wrong with your brain. You sure as hell know who I am, don't you?' I squeezed his hands.

'How could I ever forget you?' he said sadly.

I stopped laughing. I looked into his lovely, twinkling blue eyes.

I burst into a torrent of uncontrollable crying – the type that comes from your belly up. I was lost. I could think of nothing to say. My body shook from head to foot; my shoulders heaved.

I had a physical stabbing pain right in the centre of my chest, and realised that this was what people meant when they referred to 'a broken heart'. I sobbed like a baby, rocking my beloved friend on the tiny bed. He spoke slowly, collecting his thoughts, choosing his words carefully, his voice barely audible. At times, he paused, trying to catch his breath. Other times, his mind wandered, and he spoke of people I knew nothing about. I knew it was the medication making him groggy and confused, but such was his concentrated effort to get out what he needed to say, I was able to distinguish what was meant for me from what wasn't. I wanted to lay my head on his chest, but his body was so fragile. His ribs and breastbone protruded through his skin, and I was afraid I would crush what was left of him if I applied any pressure.

'The kids? Bet they can't wait for the holiday?' he rasped.

The holiday. It was the last thing on my mind. I was heading to Trabolgan with the kids in two days. It was to be our first real family holiday. The kids were so looking forward to it. They were ecstatic at the thought of the journey alone. I tried to join in with their enthusiasm, packing for days, as if we were going to Thailand for a month. It was just a three-day trip to County Cork.

'Charlie, I'll cancel it. We can go some other time.'

'No, no,' he insisted emphatically. 'You must go.'

'I can't,' I wept.

'I'll never forgive you if you don't. You can't let those children down now. You must go. I am *telling* you to go, not asking you,' he barked. The quandary I found myself in was unspeakable. Even at this point, Charlie was thinking of everyone else and not himself.

'I'll go. I'll go. Hush now. Don't be upsetting yourself.' I stroked his head affectionately. It was the first time I had ever seen Charlie in real pain. His jaws were clamped tight, rigid with discomfort. If I could have dug my hands inside his body and pulled the pain out, I would have.

'This,' he said, pointing to his body, 'is just a carcass. A vessel for the soul. It's nothing more, and you must believe that.'

'Charlie, don't.'

'This dies, but I do not. This is nothing but a shell. God gave it to me for a loan while I was on this earth. Now he wants to take it back. But my spirit, my soul – me, Charlie, he goes on.'

I choked.

'Your job now is to make sure that that spirit goes on in you, as you live out the rest of your life. Remember me for what I did, and not what I said. That is all I ever wanted.'

'I understand,' I sobbed.

'Tell me what you learned?'

'Where do I begin?'

'At the beginning.'

'I learned that life happens. I learned that to forgive others is to forgive myself. I learned that happiness is an attitude. I learned that everything changes – that is the nature of life. I learned that I am supposed to be flawed. I learned to listen more. I learned I can trust myself better than anyone else. I learned that when I am honest, I am strong. I learned that I know nothing about true love.'

'Keep filling them in.'

'I don't understand.'

'I'm not going away for ever.'

'I know, sweetheart, I know.'

'Just on a little trip.' He giggled all of a sudden, like a giddy, skittish two-year-old. 'Come fly with me, let's fly, let's fly away,' he hummed.

I hummed along with him.

'All of life, all its seconds, minutes, hours, weeks, months, years, all of it brings us here, all of us come back here, all of us come home. Home sweet home. If you could see what I am seeing, you would never worry or fret. We waste our lives wanting. Peace is being free of one's self. We enslave ourselves. We are our own prisoners. I never knew what God was all that time. Fifty-six years of not knowing, not understanding.

God is this. God is this. Pure, unadulterated, unconditional love.'

His words came out in dribs and drabs. I never had to listen so hard in all my life.

'Charlie, rest.'

'Rest? I have eternity to rest,' he smiled, his eyes closed now.

'Keep writing. Remember what I said. Five years. It must be five years now. You will be discovered. Soon. I know it in my heart. I will be there with you on that day.'

I buried my head in his hands and kissed them.

'How can I ever thank you for all you have done for me?' I wept inconsolably now.

'When your first novel is published, make it a gift to me. That can be your "thank you" gift.'

'I'll do that,' I promised.

'No more blanks, no more blanks.'

'What, sweetheart?'

'Fill your cap with dreams, and don't waste a second wondering if they will happen. Go after them. Don't push your children to succeed in the material world. If they are content in their own skin, they have already succeeded. If you follow your dreams, they will too.'

'OK.'

'Take my book of poems. It's on the locker. I am entrusting

it to you. Do what you will with it.'

'I will.'

'No more blanks, Cath. The job is done.'

I didn't understand him, and it didn't matter.

'Where is "Sob"?'

'He's at home.'

'Keep him by you always.'

'I will.'

'I want no wailing at my funeral. Celebrate. Laugh. Wear bright colours. I have had a wonderful life. I got a second shot at it. God blessed me.'

'I know.'

'Fill them in. Fill in those blanks and know you are, and you always will be, loved, beyond and above. I am always here to talk to, always here, always at your side.'

Charlie closed his eyes.

I lay there cradling him, crying like a baby.

We went to Trabolgan. Don't ask me how I did it. I was in some strange, robotic hypnosis. Like someone else was doing the doing for me. Just before I left the house, I caught a glimpse of 'Sob'. He was sitting on top of my typewriter. I grabbed him and stuffed him into my bag. It was the only piece of Charlie I had to take with me.

I knew it was not my place to phone his family and hassle them for details. It was Charlie's time to be alone with his loved ones. His family meant everything to him, and I knew that. My other AA friend, whom Charlie sponsored, stayed behind. She kept me up to date by phone, making regular calls to me. Soon after I left, Charlie fell into a deep coma. I understand that this was brought on by a large increase in morphine administration. The other option was to leave him in agony, and to do so would have been cruel and inhumane.

In Trabolgan, I tried to see to it that the kids got their holiday, as promised. It was the last place on earth I wanted to be. Thank God, it was such a hive of activity that I was required to do very little but supervise their amusement. They took to Trabolgan's famous swimming pool for hours at a time, and were entertained with games, competitions and club meetings in between. I sat on the sidelines, my fake smile glued on, my hand waving encouragement, as they took part in all kinds of fantastic frolics. I felt dead from the inside out.

On the Wednesday morning, my phone rang, and I knew before I even answered it that Charlie had passed away. I had been sitting on my bed with Sob on my lap, and squeezing his right hand and listening to his comical little ditty: 'Old MacDonald had a farm, ee-iy-ee-iy-oh'. Just before the phone rang, the childish jingle slowed to a drone, then stopped working altogether. The battery had died.

Seconds later, I learned that Charlie had never regained consciousness, and had slipped away quietly in the early hours of the fourth of September 2000. The funeral was held two days later. This gave me just enough time to get back to Dublin. I attended, dressed in a white dress and sandals, along with a plethora of family, friends and other AA members, paying their respects. It was only when I actually saw the coffin, and a family member sombrely place Charlie's favourite hat on top of it, that the reality sunk in. Charlie was gone. Charlie was gone for ever, and I would never see him or speak to him again. Charlie was cremated in Glasnevin Cemetery, and his ashes were retained by the family. That evening, I took out the bound book of his work, and thumbed through it till I reached the poem 'The Crossword Girl'. I read it out aloud to myself, and only then did I understand what he had been trying to say the last time we had spoken together.

'Fill in the blanks; no more blanks.'

Perhaps he hoped that he had been responsible for filling in some of those blanks by taking the time to help me in my journey? Or maybe he just meant for me to keep on living and fill them in myself? Either way, the core message was clear. It was a wish and a blessing that I might fulfil my promise to him, to God, and mostly to myself, to participate fully in the business of living, as best I could, without him.

Charlie has continued to guide me, help me, inspire me, and be by my side. Sometimes I think he has helped me more since he passed away. I have had extraordinary experiences in relation to Charlie since he left this world. He pops up all the time, making his presence known in as varied and as comical a way as he did when he was alive. He has a particular fondness for doing this when I get myself into trouble or am feeling low. I don't think I could even begin to recount these occasions here. Perhaps that is another book altogether. For now, I hope that in the time it took for you to read this one, Charlie's words, wisdom, wit and compassion came alive again just one more time. For me, though – well, he never died anyway.

Acknowledgements

My gratitude to Peter Sheridan, who championed this book all the way. Also to Jonathan Williams for keeping the faith. My thanks also to Edwin Higel, Daniel Bolger, Karen O'Donoghue and all the staff at New Island Books their for help and support.